Awakening
Exposing the Voice of the Mosaic Mind

Mark Waller

WingSpan Press

Published by WingSpan Press, Livermore, CA
www.wingspanpress.com

The WingSpan name, logo and colophon are the trademarks of WingSpan Publishing.

EAN 1-978-59594-119-0
ISBN 1-59594-119-3

First edition 2007

Library of Congress Control Number 2006937919

Epigraph

"Awake Living Joy is within you, whether you are conscious or not. Before you awaken, it is experienced from time to time, when thought is suspended. This suspension is a portal to the Joy of Being. If thought remains suspended, *Awake Living Joy* emerges as a conscious reality in your life and you are Awake in the dream."

- Katie Davis

Table of Contents

Table of Figures

THIS BOOK IS DEDICATED WITH MUCH LOVE AND FONDNESS
TO MY TWO DAUGHTERS:
PETRA ERLANDSON AND DR. ABIGAIL WILSON

Acknowledgments

Saying "thank you" to a lifetime of contributors to one's learning is a daunting task. This is especially difficult for a therapist, as I have to keep the names of my clients confidential. My two greatest teachers have been my relationships and my clients. Therefore, I have to thank my clients, many of whom became supporters of this work—as well as my teachers as we labored in the therapy room together.

Spiritual teachers have been an important part of my life. The first was Beth O'Connor. She was instrumental in directing my attention to those parts of me that I needed to see. She also helped me find my passion for growth and learning. Thanks also goes to Dr. Richard Young, who has been a friend and mentor both personally in my spiritual walk and in my profession. He has encouraged me and always shown an interest. His comments about the manuscript were invaluable. Finally, to Katie Davis; our e-mails served to challenge my assumptions and continued to point me to the deepest truth. Her book, *Awake Living Joy,* and our dialogues that followed its reading showed me a structure to truth that no one else had revealed. This allowed me to move forward rapidly in my understanding.

I would like to thank Paul Cash for his fine work at editing the manuscript. I would also like to acknowledge those who read the earlier manuscript versions and made comments which were invaluable; Amy Garcia, Karen Martin, Petra Erlandson, Sharon Newton, Dr. John Ingram, Dr. Stan Harris, and especially Lisa Booth.

Finally, I want to express my fond gratitude and love to my wife, Sheila, who taught me the real value of watching every thought.

Preface: How to Use This Book and Why I Wrote It

Actually, you won't have to *use* this book – it will *use* you. Now, I'm being a bit facetious, of course, about the book using you. Alternating chapters contain imaginary dialogues with my psychotherapy clients. Please do the exercises right along with my clients as they do them. All the needed instructions are contained within those chapters. Follow them step by step and make them your own.

The genesis of this work and this book came after years of reading and studying. The literature on enlightenment and self-realization talks incessantly about the mind and thought, and for good reason. It occurred to me one day, as I read some dialogues between enlightened teachers and students that most students have no idea what a *thought* actually is. Somewhere, there is a gigantic disconnect.

Once one has experienced some kind of awakening, the separate nature of thought is readily apparent. Maybe in Eastern schools of enlightenment it is so apparent it is not discussed or defined to any great extent.

In my own spiritual work, this came to me gradually. Of course, I knew what a thought was; but I really didn't take much time to articulate it. It seemed second nature. But as I read and studied, it became clear that every unintended thought is an opportunity to humble the ego-mind. So I set out to, as Paul says in Corinthians, "hold in captivity every thought."

As I added this to my practice, I began to share it with my clients. I remember the first two clients that I instructed in this *thought-watching* technique. Both had powerful awakening experiences and immediately found themselves outside the mind. I thought I must be on to something!

After those powerful experiences, the transition into *witness consciousness* became my first priority for every person that came into my office. The results were not just amazing, they were breathtaking. Not only was there a *knowing* that came from this perceptual awakening, but my clients became very different people in a fundamental way. In a mixed group of aspirants, those who were watching their thoughts stood out. They talked differently. They were almost totally *process-oriented*. The others went into drama every time they "shared."

While all this was blossoming in a beautiful way, I was also a practitioner of neurofeedback. Neurofeedback (NF) is a type of biofeedback that impacts the brain and is very effective for a whole host of problems including ADD, ADHD, autism, depression, and the list goes on. Since NF deals so heavily with the brain, keeping abreast of the latest research on the brain is a priority in my practice. In addition, the study of brain function figured prominently in my doctoral dissertation.

I began to look at people in my office in terms of how their brains worked, and to organize my understanding of their behavior around the latest research. When I started the preliminary work on this book I was a *brain guy* with a lot of *brain* on my mind. Then I really hit paydirt. I stumbled upon research that relates to the themes in this book, and a kaleidoscope of conclusions suddenly fell into place.

When I took the sum of my clients' experiences, coupled it with my intuitive sense of how to use new interventions and techniques, and combined all that with the information coming out of the various brain labs around the world, I realized what is meant by the mystery of the *fall of man.* No wonder my clients were having awakening experiences!

By the way, sometimes these experiences were out-of-body, mystical, unexplainable. Something very special was happening around me. For example, when this book was nearly completed, I was directing woman through an exercise that appears in chapter 15. As she completed the exercise, she reported seeing God. It was nothing short of ineffable, surprising, and a bit overwhelming to both of us.

This book celebrates the journey to awakening I have been privileged to witness in so many people who have come into my office. I want to share this with you.

Introduction

I've struggled long and hard to understand what happened that day. It all started with a blinding insight that *I took everything personally*. It doesn't sound like such a blinding insight to just say it, without a drum roll or fanfare. But that's exactly what happened. I knew something was very wrong with my life. I knew I could no longer go on. And I knew one thing more, that something was going on with me that I couldn't see.

I knew I was angry, an angry person. Somehow that was tied into the collapse of my life. But I was helpless to see the real problem. Of course, those around me had no trouble seeing it. Isn't that always the case? We're such experts on everyone else, but ourselves – that's another matter.

That's when, after months of seeking, I saw it: I took everything personally. In that instant it was like a vault was opened inside me. I saw clearly the pain, large amounts of seething pain that was underneath the anger. It was a ribbon of pain that ran from the present moment through my viscera, my mind, and far back into my past.

The next morning, it was as if a portal had opened and I was changed forever. Yes, there was an *awakening* and the sensations of an awakening. There was no fear of death. I felt completely one with the universe. Even bigger than that, I felt as if I was the universe. And the bliss, there was a feeling of "peace that passes understanding."

All that eventually passed, and I was left thinking that I was the only one who had ever passed through such an experience. Happily, I was wrong. But it would be years of integration and study before I would discover what that *awakening* really was. I had awakened to the presence of my true Self. I had

had a glimpse of a truth so vast, had I known then what I know now, it may have engulfed me and I might have disappeared.

But instead, I drifted back into the world of the ego. Changed though I was, and having the ability to *see* life differently from that moment on, I was not saved from the ravages of drama. I had no teacher, no one to tell me what had happened. More importantly, I had no one to tell me the difference between mind and awareness. So I drifted.

And yet a truth so powerful it consumed me was at work. I went back to school. I changed my profession. I wanted to help people see what I had seen. I wanted them to wake up even though I only knew a sliver of awakening.

Years passed. I became a therapist and started working with people. I began to put thoughts and observations on paper. I finally began to read. I read voraciously. Then one day I ran across a reference to a book called *I AM THAT* by some Indian person whose name could not be pronounced by my western tongue. Nevertheless, I bought the book and read it.

In an instant I realized two things: First, I could barely understand anything this Nisargadatta Maharaj said; but his words lit a flame in me that was all-consuming. Second, my experience had not been unique and it leads ultimately to a thing called *enlightenment* or *self-realization*. That was it. I had to have it, and I was "off to see the wizard." Little did I know then that *I* was the thing I was looking for; or rather, that the enlightenment I so desperately yearned for was with me all the time.

The result of the journey that began in those days led me to dozens of books and my teacher, Katie Davis, author of *AWAKE LIVING JOY*, whose gentle prodding led me to the final understanding. At this same time, I became convinced, through my study of the brain, that the literature of enlightenment could be understood by looking at the reality of brain dynamics as it is now being uncovered by leading researchers. For me East met West in blinding insight. The result is what you are holding in your hand.

This book is the culmination of my journey as a seeker and as a therapist. I have written it in such a way that you don't have to do exercises or struggle with concepts. Odd-numbered chapters are written in the setting of therapy; in them, you'll read about someone else's struggle with the concepts. Vicariously, the exercises in them will do you! Alternate chapters are didactic in nature; hopefully they'll provide all the information you need to understand what's happening to the clients I work with on a daily basis.

The therapy sessions presented here are fictional and a composite of many experiences I have had in the room with people. You'll read other's experiences as they do the exercises. You'll hear them say what you might say in a similar circumstance. You'll share in their puzzlement and amazement.

The alternate chapters serve to combine Eastern thought with Western thought. But more than that, they present the latest brain research, sifted through the reality of what a therapist encounters every day. This is very important. There is a huge gap between what the research is saying and the way people behave. This is a gap in understanding, not reality. In other words, when research says a certain part of the brain does such and such, I am able to translate that into actual behavior that I observe in a therapy session.

Through my own experiences of awakening and my understanding of brain dynamics, much of what people do has become psychologically transparent to me. The simple practice I introduce in this book breaks my clients out of their self-imposed trance state and into an awakened awareness. Sometimes I see this happen in a session, right before my eyes. It is a blessing and truly amazing to watch someone arise from a lifelong slumber. Finally, let me make it clear that I am making a distinction between *awakening* into witness consciousness and *Self- realization*. This distinction is not a matter of semantics. It is critical to understanding the process of mind that keeps us all from the Truth.

Chapter 1: Pat and Angie Return

*Enlightenment does exist. It is possible to awaken. Unbounded
freedom and joy, oneness with the Divine, awakening into a state
of timeless grace – these experiences are more common than you
know, and not far away. There is one further truth, however: They
don't last.*

Jack Kornfield

The call I got this morning has me a bit distracted. I can see my mind
wanting to speculate and travel into an imagined future to guess what's going
to happen next. Two of my former clients, Pat and Angie, have made an
appointment to come back to see me. When clients return to marriage therapy,
it can mean that things are not good. I hope this isn't the case. I notice these
recurring speculative thoughts and the temptation that comes with them to
enter into some drama about what might happen.

I love Pat and Angie. I was their therapist. Counseling was successful for
them. I would so hate to see that things have gone badly. I remember how
hard they worked to see their own unconscious patterns. It was like watching
new life be born. I see more questioning thoughts emerge in my mind. Had
Angie's anger gotten the best of her? Was Pat shutting down and retreating
from imagined conflict as he had done so many times before? Or something
worse – an affair, some tragedy? My mind paints no end of dramatic scenarios.
I refuse to identify with any of them.

Awakening

Meanwhile, I'm waiting for Rhonda and Tim to stop arguing. Not that I have anything particularly interesting to say. It's just that it's 9 o'clock on a Monday morning and I'm not as ready for all this as I might be later in the day. Or later in the week, or maybe sometime next year. In any event, I tune in to what they're saying with an eye to doing something productive with the time.

"God, Mark, your book is awesome. I mean, there are so many things I'm seeing in it. All I can say is, wow!"

Rhonda turns to me and says. "You see, that's one of my problems right now with Tim. He constantly tells me that I'm too much of a Lion, or I'm acting that way because I am a Lion. I'm at the point where I don't care if I *ever* read that book!"

I'm thinking we can't have that.

"Tim," I comment, "That seems a little condescending, doesn't it? She hasn't even read the book and already you're kind of using it against her as sort of a weapon. Can you see that?"

"I'm just trying to avoid conflict. That's what Unicorns *do*. I just don't *like* conflict."

Rhonda shrugs her shoulders. "Conflict? Where's the conflict? You're treating me like a child. I know nothing about what the book says. You're telling me I'm a 'Lion' like it's a bad word. And when I ask you about it, you just tell me to 'read the book yourself.' I don't see the conflict in this at all."

Tim smirks and says, "I just don't know what to say. I didn't mean it to come across like that. I don't even know what's going on." He leans back with a look of satisfaction on his face.

"Tim, tell me, what are you doing right now?" I ask.

"What do you mean, what am I doing?"

"Tell me what you're doing. What is your behavior right now?"

Tim is obviously embarrassed to have me confront him like this. But we've known one another for a long time and I know he respects me, so I'm guessing he'll take this seriously and look inside for an answer.

He looks up with a sober expression and says, "I'm making an excuse. I'm not taking responsibility."

"Perfect!" I exclaim. "That's perfect insight. See, this is what I love about you, Tim. You can *do* this work. Look, this isn't about right or wrong, or good or bad. It's about clearly seeing what you're doing and where it's coming from."

While I make this remark, designed to reward what he has just done and bolster his confidence, a light goes on in my head. I instantly see why he's using my book as a weapon against his wife.

2

"Tim, I know you're excited about the book. And I know you're seeing many things you've never seen before about yourself and Rhonda. But let me ask you a question: What would happen if you just opened up to her and said, 'I'm excited about what I'm reading. Can I share it with you'?"

"I've tried that, it doesn't work."

"Alright. But let's say you did really let her know you were excited and wanted to share it, what are you afraid might happen?"

Tim thinks for a moment and responds, "She would put me down. She would just make fun of me. She wouldn't take it seriously."

"Good, so she's going to make fun of you. How will that make you feel?"

Tim's face suddenly flushes and there is a long silence in the room. He looks at me and says, "I need to take a break, just to get my thoughts together."

In the very few minutes we've been talking, my questions have led him dangerously close to an enormous well of pain that he doesn't want to feel. "No Tim, don't let yourself off the hook, not now. We're very close to something very big here, and I want you to see what it is."

"My mind is just blank right now. I can't think."

"I understand. So rather than trying to answer my questions, let me just tell you how it feels when she won't take you seriously."

"Okay," he answers.

Now, I'm taking a bit of a risk here. Normally I'd be relentless until Tim owned the feeling that he's afraid to feel. But I think it's pointless to back him into a corner. In most cases when the client is too threatened to access the feeling, I would wait until another day. But I've worked with Tim before, and during individual therapy he broke through into a level of self-observation that allows him to see what his mind is doing to him. I'm banking that his heightened insight will give him the "ah-ha!" that normally comes from breaking through defenses into the underlying pain.

"Tim, the feeling you're blanking on is embarrassment. Isn't that it?"

His eyes go wide. "That's it!" I glance at his wife, Rhonda. Fortunately, she's figured out that I'm "doing therapy" and not attacking her. She is quiet and attentive as opposed to taking Tim's distortions as personal attacks.

"Okay, then let me ask you the next important question. If you get excited about something and want to share it with Rhonda, and she just puts you down and you feel embarrassed, what does that tell you about what she's thinking or feeling about you?"

"You mean, how do I feel or how does she feel?"

"You need to kind of read her mind. You're getting excited and want to

3

share, and all she does is embarrass you for what you're saying. What does that tell you about what she's thinking or feeling about you?"

He looks at me questioningly. "That she thinks I'm stupid?"

"Yes, she thinks you're stupid. And Tim, can't you see that's the setup in the relationship—you play the role of the stupid one?"

"Yeah, I see that."

"Okay, last question. What images or memories come to mind about being embarrassed?" From our previous work, I remember the answer to this. The question is can Tim connect the dots.

He thinks for a moment and then his head drops, "My mom."

That's what I remember, too. His mom was merciless in poking fun at him and throwing water on anything about which he was enthusiastic.

"So what happens is that as soon as you get excited about an idea you're having, that fear of being embarrassed comes up. Then as fast as your mind can work, you shift into a defense so as not to feel the fear. The result is that your comment about what you want to share gets reduced to a defensive, arrogant barb that feels like an attack to your wife."

"Oh, my God, you're right."

"Tim, is it possible that Rhonda is exactly the right person to play the role of your mother? I mean, do you think it's possible that when you met Rhonda, at some level you instinctively knew that she had just the right emotional makeup and defensive behaviors that you could see her as your mother?"

Tim mulls that over and says, "Well, so many people do say that you marry your mother, or at least someone like your mother."

"Yes, I understand that's a popular belief. But I'm drawing a distinction here. I'm saying you married someone *you could see as your mother*."

"I'm not quite sure I understand what you're getting at. It sounds like the same thing to me."

"Sorry for the confusion. Let me explain. I know it must sound like I'm parsing words, but consider this. When we're about four years old, our developmental task is to have our first 'social' relationship. This isn't the bonding that happens with the mother during the early attachment phase. This is one person to another in a relationship. We then pick either our mother or our father for that first relationship, or we might pick a grandmother or some other person if we're in a nontraditional family unit. Well, this relationship is never perfect and a woundedness is the result. In other words, our needs are not met in quite the way we expected them to be. Our emotional needs are in some way unmet.

Now at that age we assume that there's no way our mother or father could be responsible, so we assume that we're the one with the problem.

For Unicorns, the problem is framed as, 'How do I get safe with this volatile person who appears to want to control me?' For Lions, the problem is framed as, 'How do I get approval from this person who is emotionally unavailable or rejecting?' We then set off to solve the problem. We develop a strategy that is set into motion to correct the problem and get our unmet needs fulfilled. The struggle begins.

This becomes wired into a primitive part of the brain called the limbic system. When we get into a committed relationship, the limbic system thinks we're back in that original relationship with mom or dad. The process of selecting a partner is directly related to finding someone who fits the picture, so the struggle can continue."

Tim looks a bit confused and interjects, "But when we first met, it wasn't like that. We didn't have any of the problems we do now."

"Right, you're absolutely right. It takes time for us to coach one another into the roles we need played to continue the struggle. So the two people who met and fell in love are still available. But they've been pushed aside by our primitive need to fix the problem of that early, original relationship with mom or dad or whoever that first social relationship involved."

"So how do we 'coach' one another into these roles?" Rhonda asks with a slightly skeptical tone.

I take a deep breath and notice a slight resistance arise in my mind. As I notice it, it evaporates. "We do a lot of it nonverbally, subconsciously. But primarily it's done through our defensive reactions. For a Unicorn, the defense is a lot of avoidance and passive, angry resistance. This always 'looks' to Lions like the disapproving, unavailable parent we knew so long ago. On the other hand, a Lion's defense is anger, which 'looks' like the out of control parent that wanted to pressure a little Unicorn to be a certain way."

So at one level, the *Dance of the Lion and the Unicorn* looks like a cauldron of effort at getting the other person to stop this behavior that brings up our pain and leaves us feeling attacked. But at the next level down, we are actually coaching and prompting the person to be in exactly that role, so we can continue the struggle we're so familiar with at an emotional level."

"That's sick!" exclaims Tim.

Rhonda shakes her head. "Oh, my God!"

"The ego-mind, the conditioned mind, is dangerously insane and completely out of touch with reality. That's a subject for later."

I pause for a moment to let that comment sink in. Then I continue, "In psychology there's a term called *ritualistic reenactment*. It means that the things we do in our adult lives are often a repeat of a pattern from the past. Our father washed the car every Sunday. We wash the car every Sunday. There is

5

another term that refers to this tendency which is *repetition compulsion*. But those two terms as they are understood don't come close to the magnitude of what actually happens to us all. I'm saying that our entire relationship is a ritualistic reenactment—that moment by moment our automatic, emotional brain is trying to solve the problem of the past. We are literally in a trance, sound asleep, only pretending to be awake. While our limbic system has us in this trance, our adult brain is saying, 'Life sucks. Why is this happening to me? I don't want to live like this!'"

Tim thinks for a moment, and then looks at me, "You mean we think we don't want what is so bad in the relationship, but at the same time we're trying to get more of it?"

"Right," I reply, "Unicorns think they don't want to live with this angry demanding person, but in point of fact, they wouldn't know how to live otherwise. The struggle puts them in their comfort zone. Lions think they don't want to live with someone who is rejecting and unavailable, but this puts them directly into the struggle for approval, which is about all they know. The bottom line is we are addicted to the *struggle*. We think we want safety or approval, but what we really want is struggle. In order to struggle, we marshal all of our resources. It's what we do best."

"Okay, so how do we get out of the struggle?" asks Rhonda.

"In concept, it's simple. We need to see how we do the struggle. We need to use our own awareness to see struggle operating in our minds. It's like a prison. How do we get out of prison? By seeing that we're not only the prisoner, but also the jailor. We need to see how we keep putting ourselves in prison."

#

I'm sitting, waiting for Pat and Angie. I'm noticing my mind playing out all the scenarios that might be prompting their visit. I hope things aren't going badly for them. They left therapy on such a high note that it would be tragic to see them backslide into the endless Dance of the Lion and the Unicorn they were in before.

They enter the room and sit in their "normal" positions that I remember so well from our past work. I try to read their faces to see what kind of train wreck might lie ahead. Then I notice that my ego-mind has made a judgment about what might happen and I smile ruefully inside to myself. My mind squirms back and forth from the remembered past to the imagined future.

Oh, to be free of the squirming of the programmed, conditioned, primitive ego-mind!

"So, it's so nice to see you both. How can I help?"

Pat suddenly looks like he's going to burst into tears. I can see him struggling to get himself under better emotional control. "Dr. Mark, please help me get the feeling back. It was so good and now I'm so lost!"

"What feeling are you talking about, Pat?"

"I don't know how to describe it. It was several days ago. I got up in the morning and felt like I was a different person. My mind was quiet and I felt this overwhelming peace. It was like a feeling of bliss. Oh, my God! It felt so good. But the next day it left. I feel lousy, like my old self again. Please, please help me get that feeling back!"

"It told him," interjects Angie, "that the feeling comes and goes. At least it does for me."

I look at her with mild surprise. "So you feel the peace, too?"

"Oh yes, it went along with that feeling of being 'reborn' that I told you about before. It didn't last all that long. Maybe a couple days. But the ability to 'see' clearly, that stayed. I never lost that. Come to think of it, I need to ask you more about that."

I turn to Pat. "Tell me, Pat, was there anything that led up to this feeling of peace? Or did it just suddenly occur?"

Pat gets a thoughtful look on his face. "Well, the last time I was here I was telling you that I was seeing my Unicorn patterns. You know, going away emotionally, shutting down, avoiding. I could see the underlying anxiety that drove those behaviors. I guess I sort of assumed that I had it all figured out. That was a big mistake, because about a month ago we had a big argument and I had to take another look at myself. Sure enough, Angie was right. I was up to my old tricks. I could clearly see what I was doing. I was shutting down and staying shut down as a way of punishing her."

"He was great!" Angie pipes up, "He came to me and took complete responsibility. It was very healing. We went on as if nothing had happened."

"Thanks, sweetie. I appreciate that acknowledgement." Pat turns to me and says, "Well, that experience was somewhat jarring for me. What you told me is so true. The passive strategy in a relationship is just as hostile as the angry strategy. I realized that maybe I had gotten a little arrogant and lazy about my new 'insight.' I vowed to work even harder to watch what I was doing. And I did. Wow! Everything got clearer and clearer. Pretty soon I was seeing not only what I was up to but what everyone else was doing, too. I got so I could see their fear or shame almost immediately.

Anyway, that's when it happened. I woke up in this state of peace and utter happiness. I felt like I was in heaven, as if I had arrived spiritually; and then it all went away. After all you've done for us, I thought you might be able to help, or at least explain what's going on with me."

I take a moment to let silence settle over the room. Pat and Angie are looking at me expectantly, but what I want more than anything right now is stillness. So I let the moment linger for a little bit longer. What has happened here is monumental. And even though both Pat and Angie are experiencing a miracle, it's important to prepare them for the journey ahead. For what has happened is that a doorway has been opened in their lives. They must not stop now. They must keep walking. Whatever I say must inspire them to keep moving ahead.

"What has happened to both of you is that you've moved to a new level of consciousness. Before you think I'm getting New Age-y on you or trying to convert you to an eastern religion, hear me out. It's important that you understand what has happened so you can continue to practice and deepen the experience of this awakening that has taken place."

Angie looks at me and says, "I think I already know what you mean. This new level is like an awareness isn't it? Like an awareness that wasn't there before."

"Yes, that's exactly right. And Pat, I'm sorry to say that grasping after the experience and feelings of it is a blind alley."

"What do you mean?" he asks.

"What I mean is that it's like when you're very hungry and you finally sit down to a wonderful meal. In the end, you feel satiated, there's a sense of satisfaction and well-being. That's not the important part of the meal. What's crucial about eating is the nourishment, not the feeling of repletion. If you become addicted to the sensations of eating, you become a glutton. If you become addicted to the sensations that accompany becoming conscious, you go unconscious in the pursuit of the experience instead of the awareness."

Pat was reluctant to let go of his powerful experience. He remained adamant that he wanted to pursue the feeling of ineffable peace he had experienced. The two of us went back and forth until a new thought occurred to me.

"Pat, let me explain something I neglected to say." He nodded and I continued, "You remember the story of Adam and Eve (Genesis 3) and how before the Fall of Man they were in Paradise?"

"Yes, I remember."

"Well, we all are struggling with our fallen nature, aren't we? We live in this state of misery. We lack peace and fulfillment, and ultimate happiness. We think there's more to life but we can't seem to find it, right?"

"That makes sense. That's the way I felt before all this took place."

"Me too," says Angie.

"Okay, so when Adam and Eve were in paradise they were in their natural state, or native state. We might infer from other sacred writings and other scriptures that they were *one* with God, whoever God is, and they experienced no pain or suffering or sense of separation. In other words, they were not only in paradise, they experienced paradise as being inside of them."

All of a sudden, Angie gets this look of recognition on her face. I look at her and acknowledge that. "Yes, that's what you both experienced. You experienced that native, natural state. Some might call the 'natural' state *enlightenment* or *self-realization*. So in essence, what has happened to both of you, and especially you, Pat, is that you have had a taste or a glimpse of that natural state."

"Oh, my God, that's exactly what happened. It must have been," gasps Angie.

I can see that the truth of what I just said is resonating with both of them. They had never put it in that context before. Having reframed their experience, they can see what it truly was.

Pat's persistence is amazing and he says, "Yes, but I still want that feeling!"

"Okay, Pat. I want it, too. I hunger for it every day myself. I'm not suggesting that you deny the yearning of your heart. But let me go back to the metaphor of Adam and Eve one more time. So the objective of humankind is to get back to paradise right?"

They both nod their heads.

"So we must get back to paradise, and when we arrive we will spontaneously feel those feelings again. They will emerge from within us as a function of the new place in which we find ourselves. But we will never find those feelings outside of the Garden. So we must journey back to the source of our fulfillment, rather than to try to re-enact the experience of being there without having actually arrived there. Does that make sense?"

Angie nods and Pat looks somewhat confused. "Okay, let me put it another way. You started to carefully watch what you were doing, right?"

Pat nods.

"What happened was that in the act of watching, your mind's 'thinkingness' suddenly came to a stop. In that moment of silence, what was already inside of you, or some aspect of the real you, suddenly emerged as the mind quieted. That peace and joy was always there, always inside you. It wasn't something you acquired. To put it another way, it's who you really are. Now the problem of how to recover it comes up. If who you are

9

is that peace, it's not something that can be acquired. That would be like a fish trying to find water. You are that peace. The problem is, you believe it's something to be found."

"Okay, so what do I do?" asks Pat.

"Ironically, it turns out that there are pointers everywhere. Everything in our lives points to the truth of our real being if we will only look." I gesture to Angie. "The biggest pointer is right here in front of you."

"Angie points to my true self where that peace is?"

"Yes, all of us in intimate relationships have been sent a teacher. It's the Lion or Unicorn we're living with."

Pat fidgets in his chair. "So she's my teacher."

I hold up my hand. "Now, don't get the wrong idea. You're her teacher, too. The teaching doesn't come in the form of great pearls of wisdom from the other person. The teaching comes in the form of what comes up inside of us in the course of day-to-day living with this person."

"You mean like our issues and baggage, like you told us when we first came to see you." Angie interjects.

"That's right, Angie. Here's the principle: Our emotional reactions, especially those we have that are triggered by our partner, tell us nothing about the other person. They only tell us about ourselves. Now, if you consider this in the context of your spiritual experience of peace, and your yearning to get back to that feeling, the relationship becomes a spiritual practice. This is so because our ego-mind, that limbic system that runs our lives, becomes the most active around our mates. And it is that, with all of its illusions and tricks, that keeps us from the full inheritance, from that natural state."

As Pat and Angie leave I notice that Pat is not completely satisfied. I can't really blame him. Entering into the peace that passes understanding is like drinking an elixir of immortality. You want more. Ironically, when we try hard to get another sip from the Source, the *trying* itself moves us further away.

Chapter 2: The *Dance and Awakening*; an Overview of Relational Dynamics

For the mature person, the Tao begins in the relationships between a man and a woman, and ends in the vastness of the universe.

Tzu-ssu

This chapter serves to summarize the main points in my earlier work, *The Dance of the Lion and the Unicorn*. Not everything there will be encapsulated in this chapter. For instance our biology or inborn temperament determines whether or not we are Lions or Unicorns, but I will leave that detailed discussion for those interested in my previous book. However, what I do want to do is to lay a context for what happens in a relationship, so that the main idea of this book can be seen against that backdrop.

This reminds me of a question I got recently at an event at which I was the guest speaker. After hearing in detail the dichotomy of the Lion and the Unicorn, one person asked if the objective was to marry or pair up with the same type rather than opposite types as so often happens. My answer was succinct. The objective is not to change the pairing of opposites. The objective is to become conscious. What a revelation!

So *The Dance of the Lion and the Unicorn* is a dance in a dream state of unconsciousness. It is a circular causal process, which is initiated by a deep trance left over from our inborn nature and early childhood conditioning. *The Dance of the Lion and the Unicorn* is a road map out of the deep sleep that results.

To simplify seeing this, I break the pattern down into three basic levels. The first is the dance itself, which we will illustrate next. This is happening at the surface level of the relationship. The next level is the level of projection. This is the level at which we activate the hidden agenda of disowned parts. It turns out, as we shall see, that a Lion has a distinctive disowned part, as does the Unicorn. This disowned quality is then projected onto our partner and, when we see it, we immediately attack it since we don't want to see it in ourselves. The final and deepest level of relational dynamics is that of *the struggle*. Here we learn that what we think we wanted all along wasn't it! As we shall see, what we really want is to struggle for it.

Finally, all these things are mere pointers to the truth of who we are. That is the point of this book – learning to see the pointers, especially those in relationships. We are being called home to the truth. By following the pointers, the truth emerges into the space left behind when we awaken to the *dance*.

THE DANCE OF THE LION AND THE UNICORN

The Dance is a dance of pain and the defenses around that pain. As Figure 2-1 shows, it has the quality of circular causality.

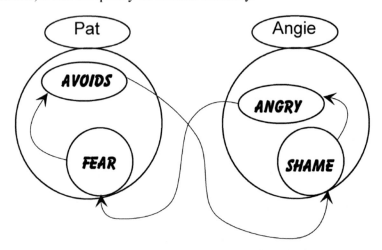

Figure 2-1 The Dance of the Lion and the Unicorn

This graphic depicts the couple featured in *The Dance of the Lion and the Unicorn,* Pat and Angie. Pat is the Unicorn. When he feels threatened (*fear,* bottom of left large circle), he retreats to *avoid* what he perceives will be a coming conflict with Angie. When Angie sees this avoidance, she interprets it to be a form of personal rejection and condemnation. She feels unloved, not special or important. She sees Pat's defense as *shaming* her. She defends her pain, the shame, with *anger*, trying to get Pat to get closer to her. This only perpetuates the cycle and around, and around it goes.

The tragedy of this is that the two people who met and fell in love are still available. This is actually a ritualistic reenactment of an earlier pattern that was centered on a parental relationship. For each person, the large circle represents the limbic system and its chaotic basin of strange attractors that help us perceive the world without really looking ourselves. This is the automatic, self-preserving part of the brain, which operates from emotional memory. As such, it struggles to resolve the problem of the pain of that early relationship.

At about four years of age, give or take, our developmental task is to engage in our first social relationship. To learn what relationships are all about, we pick one of our parents to be "the relationship." This may not always be so if we were raised by grandparents or an older sibling, in which case that person will become "the relationship." In any event, this relationship never goes quite the way we planned. Sometimes this is because of the distorted view of a four-year-old. Sometimes it is because of circumstances—say a father must travel extensively. Sometimes parental neglect or even the tragedy of abuse is involved. More often, it's a combination of one or more of these.

Also, verbal cues play an important part in this developmental process. Parents often deliver the wrong messages for a child's temperament. If the child is a Unicorn by nature, it's not unusual for a parent to use pressure and coercion to try to get a more demonstrative response from a timid and cautious child. If the child is a Lion by nature, parents resort, more often than not, to tactics that are shaming and restrictive. Since these attempts at parenting run counter to temperament, they are bound to backfire. Coerce a Unicorn and you will get a child even more wary of social contact. Shame a Lion and you are reinforcing the child's defiance and asking for a power struggle.

No matter the health or dysfunction of this early relationship, the child sets out to solve the problem of the pain of this fear or shame. The limbic system organizes around the problem, and defensive strategies are developed to cope with the ongoing atmosphere of struggle. The Lion develops coping strategies and an active defense, while the Unicorn develops coping strategies and a passive defense. The limbic system then hijacks the entire brain at any given time, throughout a person's life, in order to serve this agenda.

What about the prefrontal cortex? The prefrontal cortex is that part of the brain depicted by the small circles on the top part of Figure 2-1 with Pat and Angie's names inside. Many researchers say that the jobs of the prefrontal area, which is behind the forehead and eyebrows, are planning and decision-making. It is considered the adult brain. In *The Dance of the Lion and the Unicorn*, I refer to the prefrontal lobes as that part of the brain that is capable of self-observation. I called it the "meta-self." Since then, my view and knowledge of this extremely vital part of the brain has been enhanced. I have reduced its function, for my purposes, to a more understandable and, I believe, more dynamic term – "the watcher." What I mean by "the watcher" is a subtext for this entire book. My understanding of what *watching* actually includes has grown and become more complete. The prefrontal lobes, therefore, are the seat of *awareness* and not of *thinking* as we have traditionally conceived it. There will be much more on this point later.

The problem with this entire brain system is that the limbic system is almost completely developed by the time we're five years of age. The prefrontal lobes are only starting rapid development by then and don't finish until we're twenty to thirty years of age. This means that the primitive emotional brain—and especially a limbic structure central to emotional tendencies called the Amygdala—holds sway over the more sophisticated structure for many years. The prefrontal cortex becomes a slave to the limbic system, which can dominate with its childlike perception and strategies at a moment's notice.

Eminent brain researcher Joseph Ledoux puts it this way:

> The connectivity of the amygdala with the neo-cortex is not symmetrical. The amygdala projects back to the neo-cortex in a much stronger sense than the neo-cortex projects to the amygdala. David Amaral has made this point from studies of primate brains. The implication is that the ability of the amygdala to control the cortex is greater than the ability of the cortex to control the amygdala. (Edge org, *A Talk With Joseph LeDoux*)

The bottom line is that when the relationship, as shown in the figure, goes on autopilot, two five-year-olds are running it. The shadow figure from that first relationship is placed over our partner and we proceed as if we're still trying to solve the problem that created our original pain. And the struggle continues!

PROJECTION OF UNWANTED PARTS

We all have parts of ourselves that we don't want to see. In some psychological literature, these disowned parts are called "the shadow." No matter what we call it, there's something fascinating about this. All Lions seem to have the same disowned part, and all Unicorns have the same disowned part.

Disowned means we don't want to see this particular personal quality. We don't want to see it because it's too threatening or objectionable. Usually this has been significantly reinforced by parental messages. Very often we get repeated, strong injunctions about what personal qualities are acceptable or not. Sometimes this information is delivered explicitly, or it may be implicit in the example set by a parent. Ironically, Unicorns and Lions sort this feedback differently and universally.

Our very survival in that early relationship with that parent becomes dependent on never allowing that disowned part of us to be seen. We learn to hate it. We learn to criticize others who have it and show it. We have opinions and philosophies built around it. Since our life partner is so exposed to us; we certainly can see our shadow in them. When we see this disowned part, it appears as an undesirable quality in our partner. We criticize them for it. We attack them. We insist they change. We may even divorce them because they keep showing us what we don't want to see.

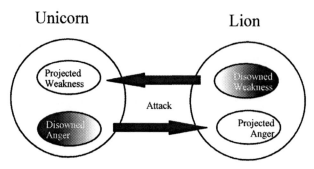

2-2 The Disowned Parts of the Lion and the Unicorn

So what are the disowned parts? For Lions, it's their weakness and vulnerability. For Unicorns, it's anger. Lions don't want to be seen as weak and vulnerable, so they project strength. They become the strong, responsible ones in the relationships. They take over everything that needs to be done. After all, they don't really believe that their Unicorn partner cares enough about them to do it anyway. Of course, by staking out this position early in the relationship, they leave no room for their partners to be seen as strong or responsible. If the Lion must be strong, the Unicorn must be the weak one. If the Lion must be the responsible one, the Unicorn must be irresponsible. And this is exactly how it usually works.

The Lion in the relationships stakes out the position of strength, thereby forcing the Unicorn's passive system to be seen as weak. Then in a master stroke of irony the Lion attacks the Unicorn for being so weak, incompetent, vulnerable, lazy – whatever. This serves the Unicorn's purposes perfectly. This attack embodies the exact quality that Unicorns never want to see in themselves, anger.

Now, despite claims to the contrary, Unicorns are extremely angry—every bit as angry as their Lion counterpart is. But by constantly goading their Lion partners into displays of rage, the Unicorn can be seen as the calm, reasonable one in the relationship. Because of this outward dichotomy, it is common for the Unicorn to sit smugly in my office, point the finger at their Lion spouse and say, "See, they're the crazy one. I'm fine. I have no problems."

The Lion then becomes the one acting out all the anger in the relationship. This gives total cover to the violence of the Unicorn's passive aggressive system, allowing them to escape the need of taking any responsibility for the dysfunction of the relationship. Their summary of the problem is simple: The relationship would be fine if their partner weren't so angry.

If you're noticing circularity and an interlocking system with disowned parts just like the *dance*, you're right. The Lion sets up the Unicorn to look weak so they can see themselves as strong. Then they attack the Unicorn for being weak. This attack looks like the crazy anger that Unicorns don't want to see in themselves, so there's an incentive for the Unicorn to be even more weak and incompetent. Why? So that their disowned anger gets projected on and acted out by the Lion. Then the Unicorn attacks the Lion for being so angry. And around and around it goes.

The Struggle

Lions want approval and Unicorns want safety. Isn't that what drives the *dance*? On the surface of the relationship, it appears that's exactly what's happening. Lions want to feel accepted, special; they want that emotional connection in the relationship. Meanwhile, Unicorns want to be close with someone who is safe. They want a relationship that's calm and peaceful. At least so it appears.

What if I told you that's all an illusion, a kind of massive self-deception? You might think I'm crazy, maybe? But if we look a little deeper into the engine that's driving all this, the limbic system, we see a four- or five-year-old child trying to solve a problem to make pain go away. However, the defensive system that has been set up to solve the problem of the pain in fact ensures that we will only get more pain. It's easy to see that the *dance* is a self-perpetuating system. We persistently do what isn't working in the hopes that things will be different. But what if things were different? What would happen then?

This is all being driven by the limbic system, and the only way the limbic system knows how to perceive is in terms of there being a problem that needs to be solved. If the problem either was solved or didn't exist, the limbic system would never notice. It lives within one tiny constricted worldview. In this world, the problem never is solved. What this means is that the system of problem-formation and struggle for resolution perpetuates itself. It is therefore all about the *struggle*. Lions, in fact, don't really want approval. What they want is the *struggle* for approval. It is all about *struggle*. Unicorns, actually, don't really want safety. They want to *struggle* for safety.

Each of these unconscious animals lives in a box where they are always measuring the distance from danger (Unicorn) or rejection (Lion) behind them moving toward the impossible goal of safety or approval that must be just ahead somewhere. The *struggle* becomes the reference point. The *struggle* becomes the road map for living. We are addicted to the *struggle* and live deeply unconscious lives striving for a goal that cannot be reached because it cannot be perceived by the primitive brain that is so mightily striving toward it.

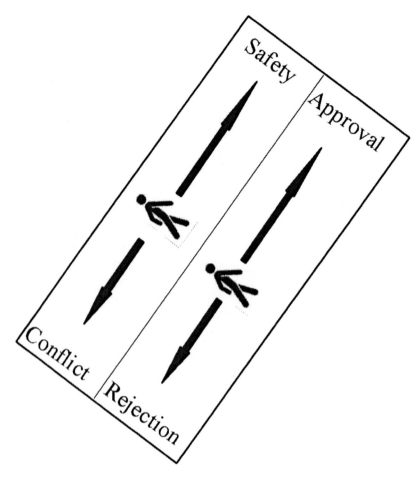

Figure 2-3 The Tiny Little Worlds of the Lion and the Unicorn

We are on the run from our pain. This addiction has us by the throat. It consumes the mind. It is hard to imagine that such a person might awaken from this trance of *struggle*. We can't have it both ways. We cannot awaken spiritually and be on the run at the same time. Some people use spiritual practice to get away from pain. They learn meditation to use the power of the mind to suppress negative feelings. They escape to a monastery to avoid the pain of close contact with others.

The purpose of spiritual practice is to relate to life in a new way, not to find something that makes us feel better. Relationships confront our fears, our shame, our anger, our devotion to the struggle of *resolving without feeling*. What better than a partner that constantly reminds us which direction to look for the blockage in our path to awakening? Relationships are spiritual practice of the most productive kind. God has sent you a teacher. It is the Lion or Unicorn you are living with.

The question then becomes can we surrender to the teaching or do we continually focus on the other person's need to change so we can feel better. It seems we are willing to climb any mountain, endure rigorous practice in uncomfortable positions, spend hours fending off sleep and hunger in silence – we will do anything for spiritual fulfillment. We will do anything, but the most difficult thing of all. Stay put, take responsibility, and master the compassion it takes to live with another person.

Chapter 3: The Paint on the Wall

*The solution is ATTENTION, attention instead of intention.
Attention to What is, in place of striving for what should be. Attention
to how things already are, without any attempt to improve them.
The fact is that total attention is surrender, and total surrender is
attention.*

Douglas Harding

The Abitinos are sitting in front of me, talking about the wisdom of one kind of retirement approach versus another. Josh Abitino is a man of medium height and rugged good looks. Genie, his wife, has raven black hair and is just downright cute from her head to her toes. But there's nothing cute about how they're talking to one another.

"He wants to put all our money in real estate. I keep telling him that real estate is too risky. What if the market bottoms out? We'll be left with nothing."

Josh leans back and grins, "Now Genie, have I ever let that happen to us? Your problem is you want all our money in a savings account. The rate of return is miniscule. Our nest egg will never grow that way." His voice has a not so slightly parental tone and I can see Genie starting to go into a slow burn.

"You see, Dr. Waller, this is the way he talks to me. He doesn't seem to understand that our savings is all we have. If he dies, I'll be left with nothing but a bunch of real estate that could be worthless. This is our retirement we're talking about. I've spent all these years raising kids and picking up after him, and now we may have nothing!"

"She thinks I'm an idiot," he tells me, "She gives me no credit at all for knowing what I'm doing."

This interchange goes on in like fashion for several minutes. Finally, I hold up my hand to intervene. "Do you understand what this conversation is really all about?"

They both look at me quizzically and say in unison, "Money!"

"No, it's not about money," I say emphatically, "You're both having strong emotional responses. Can we break this down and see if it goes any deeper than just money?"

They nod reluctantly so I can have my therapeutic moment. I turn to Genie and ask her a pointed question. "Genie, how many children were there in your family of origin?"

"As I have stated before, seven." She's a little miffed because she knows I'm doing my therapist's thing and she really doesn't want to go there. She'd rather be *right* than happy.

"Right. And what was life like when you were a little girl?"

"Like I said before, it was chaos. We never knew from one minute to the next what would happen. There were kids running around all the time. My mother was completely incapable of controlling anything. Dad worked off and on. We never knew if there would be anything to eat. Oh, and I always had to wear hand-me-downs from my sisters. I don't really remember being the original owner of anything."

"Do you think that might have made you a little more security-minded than most?"

"Well, aren't we all security-minded? Isn't that a good thing?"

So here it is. This is one of the biggest obstacles to helping people. What they're doing seems so reasonable. Why should they question it deeper? If saving money is good, why question it? If striving for perfection is good, why look deeper? If trying to keep things peaceful and calm is being good, why rock the boat to see if there's a deeper motivation? This simple fact is that "being good" is just as unconscious as "being bad." Just because my act is more socially acceptable than your act doesn't mean that it's not an act.

I look at Genie sitting there in her self-righteous defense of her "philosophy" and think that it's much better to be with someone who's real than someone who has a better "act."

"Genie, think back to those years and tell me how it felt to live in an environment like that."

"That's easy," she says, "Fear. I was in a constant state of fear."

"Do you think that might have had an impact on the way you think and look at the world?"

"I don't see how. Today we have a nice house, we live in a good neighborhood, and Josh has a good job. I'm not afraid."

"Okay, let's turn the tables. You be the therapist. I'm your client and I've come to you complaining about my wife, who has decided to quit her job as a registered nurse and sell cosmetics door-to-door. I tell you that it sounds like a 'risky gamble in an unproven business.' What would you naturally assume I'd be feeling?"

"That it was a dumb idea. It sounds like a dumb idea for sure."

"I hear you, but you're my therapist. What emotion am I experiencing as I talk about the risk involved in this kind of career transition?"

I watch Genie's expression go from a bit arrogant to puzzlement and then to amazement. "Oh my God! Am I fearful about money?"

"Before I answer that, let me pose another question. Let's pretend that it wasn't you but your daughter, Natalie, who was raised in a house with seven kids, hand-me-downs, and all the chaos and uncertainty. What impact would that have had on her?"

Genie looks at me with horror. Nothing brings emotional issues home quicker than imagining it happening to your own children. "She would be fearful."

I slide forward in my chair and look into her eyes, "No, Genie, she would have been *terrorized*. We have no real day-to-day idea of how conditions that we would consider normal impact a small, developing child. No, there was no abuse, no ill intent. But raising little vulnerable children in chaos is terrorizing."

"Yes," Genie says, "But why don't I feel it? I'm not arguing with you. It all makes sense. But why don't I feel the fear? When Josh starts talking about real estate, I just want to disagree. I don't feel the fear. But it must be there."

"You don't feel it because it's like the paint on the wall." I gesture toward the walls of my office. "Look, you didn't come in here today and say to yourself, 'Nice paint.' Yet, there's white paint covering the entire room. It's so obvious that we don't even notice it. Your conditioned mind is very much the same. This feeling of fear has been there for so many years, and it started at such a young age, that you no longer notice that it's there. And yet it's the fuel in your tank, driving the conversation about money with your husband."

Josh has been watching this interchange with a concerned look on his face. "If fear is the paint on the wall of her mind, what's my paint? I mean, what is it that's so prevalent in my world that I no longer notice it?"

I turn to him and say, "Well, let's find out. When Genie says that real estate is too risky, what does your mind tell you is happening?"

"I guess questioning my judgment would be a good way to put it."

"Okay, so when your judgment gets questioned, what meaning do you make from that? In other words, what do you think the other person is saying about you?"

Josh thinks for a minute and then says, "That I'm incompetent. It feels like I'm being put down or criticized."

"So what's the feeling that you feel along with your perception that you're being criticized?"

"I feel like I'm being put down, diminished." He pauses, and then his eyes light up. "Oh, wait, I know. It's a feeling of being unimportant, like I don't matter."

"Yes, and don't I remember from our last session that your father used to make fun of you all of the time?"

"He did," says Josh, "you know, I don't remember a time when I didn't feel unimportant."

"So in the same fashion that Genie experiences her fear, you have this sense of shame that sort of hangs as a backdrop in your mind. It has become so familiar that you don't even notice it anymore."

I let this thought sink in for a moment. Then I look at both of them and say, "So you see the conversation isn't about money or different investment techniques. It's very much about a little girl's fear and a little boy's feeling of being unimportant."

I look at Josh and ask him, "Do you want to scare that little girl?" I turn to Genie and ask, "Do you want to shame that little boy? Don't we want the hurt to stop? Isn't that why we marry one another? I don't mean that you don't ever buy real estate. I mean we need to honor the other person." I look at Josh as I gesture to Genie and continue, "This isn't about real estate. For her it's about being safe. Can you help her feel safe and secure?"

I turn to Genie and look her in the eyes, "Genie, he wants to feel admired. There's nothing wrong with that. His ideas aren't stupid. Hear him out. Don't put him down. The two most important topics in this marriage are your fear and his shame."

#

24

Pat has come in by himself to work with me. For him, the goal will always be to recapture that overwhelming peace he described in his last session. For me, the goal is slightly different. I want to introduce him to what will be, for him, a new concept.

"Now Pat, I understand you've really perfected the ability to see your Unicorn patterns."

"Right, I can literally see myself trying to go away when I feel threatened. It's definitely sort of a shutting-down feeling."

I look at him and see confidence in what he has discovered about himself. He breaks the short silence with another comment.

"There's something else I can see, too. Can I tell you what it is?"

"Of course, go ahead."

"I've seen my anger. I mean, I don't express anger openly; what I do is to just stop. I refuse to do anything. I also notice that I refuse to show any emotion. To Angie or the outside world, I look completely calm—as if nothing is bothering me."

"Yes, Pat, it's perfect that you see that. That's your passive resistance. That's the way you do battle."

"I know. I procrastinate, I slow down, and I don't show up on time. It is almost as if there's a voice in my head that says, 'Nobody tells me what to do.' So when I get angry, I just dig in my heels and refuse to budge."

I chuckle at the image of him digging in his heels. "That's very much a Unicorn pattern. It must have come as a great revelation to you that you have your own angry weapon in the battle to get your way in life."

"Obviously, I'm never going to get back that 'peace that passes understanding' if I'm passively resisting everything."

What Pat is doing right in front of me is huge. He is commenting on *process* instead of *content*. This means that he's seeing how his mind works rather than becoming involved in the drama of his thoughts. Most people never make this leap in awareness.

I confirm his experience, "Right, you can't serve two masters. This is what most people don't understand, especially spiritual people. You cannot serve your spiritual goals of fulfillment while your conditioned mind is at war with what's around you."

Pat sits back and sighs. Obviously, the preliminaries are over and he wants to get to the real work at hand, feeling the bliss again. "Okay, I'm ready. Tell me what I need to do to get back that feeling."

I smile, knowing that I'm being set up here a little bit. So I say, "Pat, you know I can't exactly do that. But I think we can start with a bit of an experiment to see if we might be able to recreate some of what you experienced."

"I understand. I wouldn't do that to you. I know it's a long shot, but I'm willing to try anything. So fire away."

"Okay, what I want you to do is to sit back and relax. Take a couple deep breaths. This experiment is going to require you to pretend."

"Alright, what should I pretend?"

"I want you to pretend that you have completely forgotten your name or any personal identity whatsoever. Pretend that you have amnesia, that you have no idea of a past or of who you are."

Pat looks at me in horror. "I don't know how to do that. How do I forget my name? Funny, I immediately felt scared."

"Yes, that fear is typical. We're removing your ego-mind from the driver's seat, and that's scary. But you'll be okay, Pat. Just go along with me. So I want you to forget any form of personal identification. Oh, and one other thing, you have no anticipated future. There's nothing to worry about, plan for, or look forward to. You're a man with no past, no name, and no future. This is just pretend, remember. I want you to imagine that you're in a state of *not knowing*."

"How long do I have to do this? I don't think I can do this very long."

"Right, you'll only be able to do it for a split second, and then you'll 'remember.' Then try again. You'll cycle through this little experiment many times in the course of a minute or so. But as you do, there will be fleeting little slices of time where you'll slip into that state of not knowing."

"Alright," Pat says. He closes his eyes and leans back in his chair. Then he opens his eyes and says, "I don't think I can do it. My mind is so busy."

I put up a hand. "Pat, just relax a little and take your time. Just pretend that you don't know your name, that you have no past or future, and see what happens."

I watch as Pat takes a deep breath and tries to calm himself. As a Unicorn, Pat has a lot of internal activity that never shows on the surface. His calm demeanor belies furious mental activity. Lions, on the other hand, are very much external in many ways. They wear their feelings on their sleeve. It takes Pat a minute or two to get into the mood. Finally, I can tell by his facial expression that he's scanning his internal experience.

From previous experience, I know that people struggle with this little exercise. Pretending to *not know* is something very foreign, and the mind wants to struggle against the very idea. But upon close inspection the pretense does work, if only for fleeting fractions of a second.

Pat opens his eyes and a smile creeps across his face. "It was there. The peace, it was there."

"Yes, the peace is there."

"Wow!" Pat is still reeling from his experience. "So does this mean that I have to forget who I am to find true peace?"

"No, Pat, it's exactly the opposite."

Pat looks at me with a quizzical expression. "Do you mean that I have to remember who I really am?"

"You're on the right track. But that would imply that you need to acquire some knowledge. In fact, that's not what really happens. In our little demonstration, nothing new was learned. The peace didn't come from anything you discovered. No effort was needed to *find* the peace. It merely emerged into the space that was left when you forgot who you were."

"Now I'm a bit confused. I said, 'I have to forget who I am to find true peace.' Then you said it was the opposite. If I don't need to forget who I am, what am I supposed to do?"

I smile and lean forward in my chair. "Pat, this may sound like I'm parsing words here. But the distinction is extremely important. If we are to be free, fulfilled, and really live full-time in that peace, we don't need to forget who we are. We need to forget who we are not!"

I notice Pat is in deep contemplation as he leaves. That tells me he is taking this all seriously and trying to look deeply into himself. I know the yearning in his heart for Truth will propel his search forward.

Chapter 4: The Watcher

Devotion is nothing more than knowing oneself.

Ramana Maharshi

Just as some really obvious things become hidden like paint on the wall, some things become too difficult to see because they're technical. This chapter is important in that it discusses the brain. Often when I do workshops and seminars, all this brain stuff gets a little heavy for some people. On the other hand, I've had discussions with brain researchers who accuse me of being too simplistic and highly speculative. Despite that, I will be somewhat technical here while making some broad generalizations. With that in mind let me plunge ahead while trying to make this as easy to understand as possible.

THE PREFRONTAL LOBES

There is a part of the brain that until recently has been a mystery to science. It has been extremely hard to analyze. That part of the brain is known as the "Prefrontal Lobes." An easy way to think of the location of this vital part of the brain is to look in a mirror. The prefrontals are right behind the forehead and extend to underneath the eyebrows.

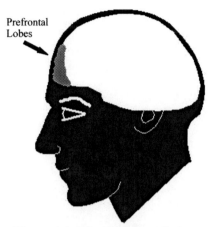

Prefrontal
Lobes

Figure 4-1: The Prefrontal Lobes

Most brain research is done on people who display deficits because of brain injury. The term for these injuries is a lesion. From studying what happens to the cognitive performance or functioning of someone who has a lesion in a certain area, inferences are made as to what that particular structure of the brain does in normal people.

A tremendous amount of information on brain functioning has been accumulated using this and other testing techniques. But that all got even better with the advent of the MRI and other highly sophisticated instruments. Now researchers can watch brain metabolism and activity in real time, thereby dramatically refining their understanding of what each area of the brain does.

Even with all this refinement, there is still much discussion as to the function of the prefrontal area. Most scientists agree that the prefrontal lobes are active in planning and decision-making. There is wide agreement that our sense of "self" is somehow predominant in the prefrontal lobes. I don't quite agree with this, and you'll see why as we go along. I believe it is more accurate to say that our sense of "being" is a function of the prefrontals. Another way to say this is as "the presence of awareness." Let me turn that inside out now and say "the awareness of presence." I say all of this to contrast this "sense" with the feeling of "me."

In other words, our sense of awareness, existence, or presence is something we experience as quite distinct from the feeling of "me" or personal identity. Later I will explain this feeling of "me" in much more detail, for it is one of the key concepts in this book.

Another vital role the prefrontals play concerns our social orientation.

Getting along with others, being socially appropriate, and having empathy for others—all are functions that literally disappear if there is damage to the prefrontal area.

One of the most famous and first-documented cases of this is that of Phineas Gage. In 1848, Phineas Gage was a man among men. A railroad foreman, he was known for his restraint and sensibilities. He was strong, athletic, and to his bosses was the most capable man they had on the job. Then one day tragedy struck.

Phineas had been placing explosive charges in bedrock to blast a straight path for the rails to be laid. Momentarily distracted, he started tamping the charge with an iron bar before his work partner was able to ply the required layer of sand. Blam! The ensuing explosion blew the iron tamping rod, which was one inch in diameter, through the underside of his left cheek, behind the eye socket and out the top of his head. The passing rod had carved out a one-inch cylinder through the prefrontal area of his brain.

Unbelievably, Gage made a full recovery, physically at least. He was not impaired in manual dexterity or his ability to walk. But sadly, the man everyone admired had disappeared. The recovered Gage was a foul-mouthed, impulsive man who couldn't behave according to the norms of society. He lost his sense of personal responsibility, couldn't focus or concentrate, and lacked basic control over his lower instincts. Such is the function of the prefrontals.

The prefrontal lobes are the inhibitory gate for the entire brain. Very few cognitive functions happen unless they pass through and get the okay from the prefrontal area. For instance, if you are going to get angry, the expressing of that or any other emotion must go through the inhibitory gate of the frontal lobes. People with poor frontal regulation have poor self-control. When we drink too much, the prefrontals are sedated and we lose our inhibitions. Poor prefrontal lobe development is implicated in many mental health issues including ADHD, autism, schizophrenia, depression, anxiety, and a host of other mental ailments.

From the viewpoint of human evolution, some scientists think that as the prefrontal lobes were the last part of the brain to form, they still may not be wired up just the way they should be. By exercising the prefrontal lobes through a form of biofeedback called HEG neurofeedback, new circuits can be built and a variety of mental health problems can be solved through enhanced performance of the prefrontals.

HEG stands for hemo-encephalography. "Hemo" stands for blood. What the person does is to attempt to increase the amount of blood flowing in the front of the brain through exercising intention and concentration. Increased blood flow increases the temperature of the forehead. One form of HEG neurofeedback uses this increase in temperature as feedback for the person doing the exercise. The result of this is that the prefrontal area is exercised and thereby strengthened; blood circulation is increased, and therefore oxygenation, profusion, and metabolism are increased.

PREFRONTAL BASIC FUNCTIONS

Other critical aspects of prefrontal performance are those of short-term memory, focused attention, concentration, and motivation. These functions really speak for themselves, but I want to emphasize attention as this will come up later in a big way. Attention is defined as the act or state of applying the mind to an object of sense or thought. We live in a sea of constant turmoil. Our senses are bombarded with input and our mind races with a cacophony of thought. Most of my clients complain that they can't get their head to shut up!

The prefrontal lobes act as our target-seeking mechanism. It is with the prefrontals that we zero in on only those things that draw our attention. We might assume that attention is an executive function under the direction of higher-order cognitive processes, guided by what is good and right in life. Ah, au contraire, mon ami. As we shall see later, this process is regularly hijacked in most critical situations!

SELF-REFERENCING

Finally, the prefrontal lobes perform a vital function which is called "self-referencing." Being self-referential means that one has turned toward one's self. We are looking inward. If I asked you to think of the name of a certain well-known political figure, for example, nearly all of us would have an immediate positive or negative reaction. If I then asked you to describe how you arrived at that reaction, you would have to go inside and look to see why you reacted the way you did. This process of looking inside to see why we react a certain way is called being self-referential. Synonyms for self-referencing are introspection, self-observation, and self-examination. In effect, then, when we look inside, we are activating the prefrontal lobes.

Sadly, the effects of childhood abuse, neglect, stress, shaming, coercion, and inconsistent parenting damage the prefrontal lobes' ability to process emotions and impulses, and to effect inhibition in general. Meanwhile, those conditions hyper-arouse the more primitive emotional signaling circuits in the brain. So the child and resulting adult gets a double whammy. On the one hand, when they are triggered emotionally, they go off the scale. On the other, their ability to put their reactions in perspective is simultaneously severely limited. In short, the more severe the child-rearing environment, the less likely it is that the person will have any ability to self-reference.

Let's see what this is like, using the above example of mentioning the prominent politician. If a person from a stressful childhood that resulted in a lack of the ability to self-observe reacted negatively to the naming of the political person, they would be unable to examine their internal process. Even the challenge to look inside would take them right back to the original reaction. This happens through association with the original reaction. It is impossible for this type of person to pull themselves out of their reactive state to do any sort of self-examination. There are numerous examples of this on daytime television every day.

For some people, this only happens when they are in the presence of their spouse or partner. Since the other person is in many cases a psychological surrogate for the original abuser, the associative emotional forces at work in the brain completely overwhelm the prefrontal lobes' ability to govern the person in the social arena. Such people completely lack the ability to talk about a situation without going right back into the drama.

Unfortunately for those of us in the helping professions, we must simply sit back helplessly and watch all this happen. Virtually anything we say or do acts as a trigger to activate the person. Their ability even to sit in the room and do any therapeutic work is lacking, as they simply cannot tolerate the emotions they experience when talking about anything painful. It is impossible to ask them a simple question without them feeling blamed or accused. They usually blow up and storm out in the first session.

By the way, since we always match up with someone at our level of pain and psychological damage, such people have an uncanny knack of finding one another. Their relationships are stormy, abusive, unstable, and filled with drama. Such is the world of compromised prefrontal lobes.

MENTALIZING

Since self-referencing and other terms like it are cumbersome and can be a little ponderous, I have come up with a term that I feel truly describes the role of the prefrontal lobes – *watching*. The prefrontals are the "watcher." As the center for awareness in the brain, they provide the nexus of watching in our minds. By "watching," I mean tuning in to what's happening inside.

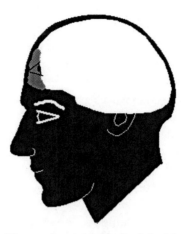

Figure 4-2: The prefrontal lobes look inside (the third eye?).

Some researchers have called this process "mentalizing." Mentalizing means the process or processes we use when we understand our own or someone else's mental process. You might call it thinking about thinking. When we think about our own or other's mental process, we activate areas scattered around the medial prefrontal cortex. This means right in the middle of the prefrontals.

Watching is mentalizing, but I want to be more specific for our purposes here. *Watching* means watching our thoughts. We use the prefrontal lobes to observe ourselves experiencing a thought.

Back to the example of the well-known politician. I might ask you to watch what your mind does when I say the politician's name. Watching or mentalizing, in this case, means observing the activity of the mind as thoughts appear and disappear, or as thoughts appear, associations are made, and the next thought in a chain of thoughts appears. It means watching any feelings or reaction to those thoughts that might happen.

When one engages in this process, we activate the prefrontals in a way that makes us feel like an outsider or third-party observer of our mind. In other words, we're not *thinking* about thinking, we're *watching* thinking.

Let me clarify something at this point that may seem confusing. Thought-forms come to us as images, sounds, voices, and feelings. Obviously, we don't watch a sound, or do we? I am using the term "watching" as a noticing of the activity of the mind. "Sensing" or "listening" are other terms I might have used. I've chosen "watching" because to me it feels closer to the idea of *awareness*. "Becoming aware" is a little awkward, so "watch" seems to fit best. See what you think as the ideas in this book unfold.

THE CHILD BRAIN

If you take your hands and feel slightly above a line from your temples to your ears on either side of the head you will feel a bulge. Underneath this are the temporal lobes. Buried inside each temporal lobe is a small almond-shaped structure called the Amygdala, which is about one inch long. The word "amygdala" means "almond shaped" in Greek. The job of the Amygdala is to regulate emotion and guide emotion-related behaviors. This sounds like one of those textbook descriptions until you realize that nearly everything we do is emotion-related. All behaviors are driven by emotion.

The Amygdala is part of a very primitive and complex set of structures called the *limbic system*. Another structure of importance in the limbic system is called the "Hippocampus." Hippocampus is a Greek word that means "seahorse." The Hippocampus is shaped a little like a seahorse that wraps around the back of the ears. It is involved in emotions, spatial orientation, and memory.

The limbic system is pretty much completely wired up by the time we are five years of age. In terms of emotional learning, it is not far from the truth to state that everything it is ever going to learn is learned by that age. So if the Amygdala is regulating and guiding emotion, the template for this is laid down by the age of five. The implications of this are very scary.

One of the critical facts that researchers have unearthed about limbic structures is that they change in keeping with what is experienced in those first critical years. In particular, the Hippocampus responds to stress chemicals by shrinking. This means that the ability of a child in an abusive environment to lay down memory and to maintain their environmental orientation is somewhat impaired when compared to a child in a non-stressful environment.

The Amygdala responds to the same set of circumstances by becoming inflamed, for lack of a better term. Emotional triggers become raw and ultra-sensitive. The result of these two factors in an adult who had a stressful childhood is someone who is always upset and can't remember why.

KEY CONCEPT

The limbic system is concerned with self-preservation, with the survival of the organism. Emotional reactions, i.e., defensiveness, are our main tools to accomplish this. These strategies of survival are wired in by five years of age. What about the prefrontal lobes that give us our humanness, compassion, and all that other good stuff? The major wiring of the prefrontal area doesn't start until about five years of age and doesn't end until we are nearly twenty; in some areas of the prefrontal cortex, that number may be as high as thirty years of age. Because of this gap in development, something untoward happens that affects the human condition and has been the source of unhappiness of humanity for eons.

In the following chapters, I will lay out exactly how this difference in development has trapped humankind in an ego-driven hell for eons. Pay close attention because the doorway out of that prison is at hand.

Chapter 5: The Conditioned Mind

The present moment is never involved in thinking. Whenever you think, you must be thinking of something from the past or something from the future.

Leonard Jacobson

Marissa is saying that she's starting to see her patterns, but it doesn't do her a lot of good. "You told me that all I had to do is to see the patterns and they would start to loosen their grip on me. Well, I'm a Lion. I know I'm a Lion. I can feel the shame that's underneath the anger. The problem is, it happens the next day. Everything is so clear the next day. Then I have to go back to Dick and apologize and take responsibility. But I just don't seem to be able to do it when it's happening in the middle of the conflict."

I understand her frustration. It's something I hear from most clients when they're starting to do the work of waking themselves up. "Don't be hard on yourself, Marissa. For heaven's sake, look at the last six months— how far you've come."

She nods her head in recognition as she put things back in somewhat of a perspective. "I guess I am a little impatient, aren't I?"

"Look, you're trying to learn a new skill. The conditioned mind has been busy co-opting your present-moment experience for, what, thirty-five years? It took me six months to convince you that it's your mind and not Dick that's the source of all the trouble."

In this moment, I remember my own struggle to awaken many years ago. There were times that conversations would simply disappear from memory. So clouded and misty is the conditioned mind that concepts outside of its distorted perception cannot penetrate. I remember on more than one occasion I needed to call a person later and ask them to repeat what they had said. I had tremendous difficulty assimilating information that didn't conform to my internal model of the world, relationships, and me.

"I just didn't want to take any responsibility. I'm not proud of that."

"Marissa, I appreciate your saying that, but the issue is much bigger. The ego-mind wants desperately to blame our partner, God, the world. We never want to look in a mirror and see what's really going on. The simple fact is that the limbic system is a five-year-old who lives in our heads and is used to hijacking the entire brain at any given moment. It has its set of triggers for which it's constantly scanning. It's prepared with a course of action. There is enormous momentum to all of this. It's a deep trance that affects our thinking and our physiology. The mist around our heads takes some time to clear."

She's shaking her head. "It should be happening faster. That's all."

As she says this, I feel the resonance of sudden recognition. "Marissa, you just went into the trance. Can you feel it?"

Her eyes get big and she looks at me. "What just happened?"

"Go inside and listen to that voice in your head that's saying, 'It should be happening faster.' Take your time."

Marissa starts shifting her eyes toward her left ear and I know she is inside her head, listening. She closes her eyes for a moment and then opens them rather suddenly. "I hear my mother. It's my mother saying it needs to happen faster."

"Right."

"But how does that happen? I don't want to hear her speaking to me like that. After all, she's been dead for ten years."

"In psychology, there is a term called an 'introject.' It means we've incorporated something into our subconscious. In this case, you have incorporated you mother's critical voice and the actual phrasing she would use into your limbic system."

I get up out of my chair and walk to the white board that's mounted on the wall. I draw a crude outline of a brain and sketch in the face of an infant inside the area of the brain.

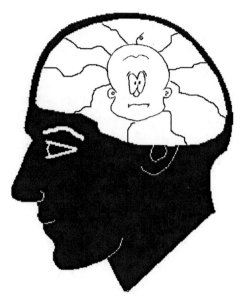

Figure 5-1: The little kid inside our head

"Here's what happens. I know I am repeating what I have said to you before. By the time we're five, the limbic system is pretty well developed and wired into the rest of the brain." I draw a series of squiggly lines extending from the child's head throughout the brain. "Now, some of these lines connect the limbic system to what are called the 'association cortexes' in the brain. The job of the association cortexes is to help the limbic system constantly pair our current experience with experiences of the past. What this means is that the primitive brain, that five-year-old in your head, is constantly scanning for what it thinks is important and reacting to it. When things don't happen fast enough, your mother's critical voice is right there just as she was when you were a little girl. So by association, your personal growth, our work together, has fallen into the generalized category of what your mother thought was 'too slow.' At least that's what got coded into your brain."

Marissa shifts a little in her chair and says, "But my mother was always a critic. Why is it only important when I was five years old or younger?"

"Well, those early memories are more of a priority in the hierarchy of survival. That early learning is more important for our instinct to preserve our lives. Later learning is more about how to get along in society, but everything is invariably linked to survival. Even when we're all dressed up in our finest evening attire, ready for a night on the town, we're still poised to survive above all else."

I take a moment to let that sink in. "It's hard for any of us to come to realize how much of our thinking is actually organized around our need to survive. Since it's so pervasive, we learn to ignore it. The problem is that your mother's behavior never changed. As a result, that early learning was constantly reinforced at higher levels of sophistication over the years. Experiences with your mother that might have countered that early learning and that would have therefore ameliorated its effects, never took place. Instead, that learning was reinforced for years.

But that first learning is what's so vital, since our entire biology is oriented toward staying alive. At that time, a massive amount of brain development is taking place. A two-year-old has twenty times more neural connections than an adult does. The learning is furious and the brain is forming new connections and trimming them at an astonishing rate."

"Yes," says Marissa, "But I'm an adult now. How can all of this be happening to me? I don't feel like a five-year-old."

"That's a good question. You feel like 'you.' You have always felt like 'you.' That 'you' feeling is ever evolving, but the changes are subtle. It's like looking in a mirror. When you were five years old, you saw 'you' looking back. As an adult, you see 'you' looking back in the mirror as well. Rarely does the thought ever come up, 'Wow! Look how I've changed.' That feeling of 'me' is so familiar that we don't question it. But, trust me, that five-year-old has long since been integrated into the feeling of 'me.'"

Marissa gets a look of surprise in her eyes. "What you're saying is that my present experience is being hijacked by a five-year-old, and I don't know it. This hijacking is so familiar and so obvious that I don't see it or feel it."

She sits back in her chair, reflecting. "So as a Lion, I have these feelings that everything is personal and I'm being rejected. I feel not good enough, so I want to accomplish everything fast so I can get my mother's approval. No wonder I'm so impatient. I want the pain to go away!"

"Yes, that's the human condition. We're trying to survive the emotional pain of childhood literally in each moment. Your conditioned, primitive mind is constantly measuring the distance between you and rejection on the one hand and acceptance on the other. You must always be somewhere in the middle to be taking that emotional measurement. This means that the ego-mind must always be recreating the problem in order to try to solve it. We must 'see' the problem to continue the struggle.

Now the sad news is that, fundamentally, it's not your mother's approval that you want."

"It's not? I thought Lions want approval. Did I not hear you correctly several weeks ago?" she asks.

"You heard just fine. What I'm saying now is a refinement, in a way. It's not approval that Lions seek; it's the 'struggle' for approval. The primitive, child brain thinks that 'struggle' is the only way to solve the problem of the pain. So we become addicted to the struggle."

I lean forward and look Marissa in the eyes. "Look, Marissa, you have a lot of evidence in your life that you are approved of. But you don't care about that. Your limbic system has a narrow focus that tells you that love and approval must come from certain places in your life and in certain ways. Yet, in many ways, it's all around you. But seeing that wouldn't reinforce the need to struggle, so you delete these things from your perception so you can stay in the struggle."

"That's sick! I don't want to do that."

"It is dangerously insane. We all do it. We marry partners who can help us do it. Then we teach our children how to do it. It's called 'unconscious living.' I have another name for it: Original Sin."

Marissa nods knowingly and asks, "Okay, but what about Unicorns? How do Unicorns do this struggle?"

"What a great question! Unicorns do it the same way that Lions do it. All you have to do is substitute danger and safety for rejection and approval. Since Unicorns are always looking for conflict, things getting out of control—in other words, danger, some threat—they're always on the move toward calm, peace, in other words safety. So those are the markers that the primitive brain lays out in each moment. They become addicted to the struggle, only it's a struggle to get safer."

"So all you have to do is look at what they're doing and you can tell which is which." She states a little tentatively.

"Unfortunately, it is not that simple. Take a 'workaholic,' for example. If the person is a Lion, they're working for approval, recognition, that type of thing. However, if they're a Unicorn, they're working hard to get safe. The behaviors look the same, but the underlying pain is different. For the Lion it's the pain of rejection, while for the Unicorn it may be the pain of the fear of rejection. Sounds similar, but the two are very different."

#

"Angie!" I exclaim. "I thought I was only seeing Pat today."

She comes in with Pat and sits down with a big grin. "So you thought you were rid of me, did you?"

I laugh. "You know better than that. You're one of the truly special people in my life. So cut that out!"

Pat pipes up. "She did that exercise that I did and she wants to ask some questions."

"Really. What happened, Angie?"

Everyone takes a seat and Angie reflects for a moment and then starts to talk. "Well, you remember when Pat came back to see you, he was talking about this extreme sense of peace. Well, I think I felt it, too."

"Really! Okay, that doesn't sound like a problem."

"All right, you said to forget your name, forget your past, and forget any imagined future. Well I did that and I felt peaceful, just like Pat did."

"Okay?" I question. She looks like a cat with a mouse in its mouth.

"So I did that and then some time later, I can't even tell you when, all of a sudden everything was okay."

I look at her questioningly. "Everything was okay?"

I could tell that Angie was struggling trying to describe something that words seemed to fail to describe.

"Everything was perfect. It was as if nothing was wrong. There was a perfection to everything. There was nothing to fix, nothing out of place. Everything was just as it was supposed to be. It's hard to describe. It was as if I was in a state of perfection and stillness. What was happening to me? It seemed like it lasted for a few minutes. But it could have lasted a few hours. There was no sense of time. Is this what heaven is supposed to be like?"

"Angie, this is what reality is supposed to be like," I opined.

Angie is still reliving the experience. "It was as if I was in another world. There was no place to go, nothing to do." Suddenly she turns to me and says, "If I had died, it wouldn't have mattered. Can you imagine that? I was very aware that I had no fear of death. Then it went away. Just like it did for Pat. What's happening to us?"

I lean back and close my eyes. In the room, nothing is moving. I can hear the tick of a clock that I surreptitiously hid on the floor next to the chairs on which Pat and Angie are sitting. I take a deep breath and start to talk.

"You both have had profound experiences and I want to explain, at least in part, what has happened. But let me emphasize that pursuing the experiences as a goal is a blind alley. So let me try to put this in a different light.

"We need to go back to the exercise and ask a basic question. There were really three parts to the exercise. First was to forget your name, second to forget the past, and third to pretend there's no future. Once we do that, what would be left?"

"I know," says Angie. 'Now.' We are left with 'now.'"

"Correct. The purpose of the exercise was to strip away a person who is thinking of the past or the future. What is left is simply 'now' without anyone doing any interpretation."

Pat leans forward, looking at the floor as if to gather his thoughts. "Do you mean that when we experience 'now' we experience that peace and that perfection?"

"That is precisely what I'm saying. What does this imply? The implication of it is that the mind is devoted to a 'me' that is either remembering the past or projecting into an imagined future."

Angie asks, "Why does everything look so perfect in the 'now'?"

"Rather than me trying to answer that, I'd prefer that you see for yourself. Let me give you an example of what's really happening.

"Let's pretend you're standing in a forest, looking at a large pine tree standing by itself in a clearing. The experience is overwhelming. The perfection of the tree, its beauty, its energy envelops you. Then you start thinking and ask yourself, 'Is this a lodgepole pine or a ponderosa pine?' Now you're no longer experiencing the tree, you're experiencing an analysis of the tree. Ask yourself, does the thought 'pine tree' smell like a pine tree? Is there a tactile feeling that goes with the thought 'pine tree'? When we're in our heads, we are experiencing thought. But if all the thoughts are about associations and projections, we're in either the remembered past or the imagined future. We are never really here, now."

Pat pipes up, "But I have plenty of thoughts about the present moment."

"I understand why you would say that. But if you analyze each thought as it arises in consciousness, you'll see that they're all linked with an association with something from the past. The imagined future is merely the past projected forward. So prove it for yourself."

"So when we are so-called 'lost in thought,' we're not in the present moment," Angie concludes.

"Right," I reply. "Consider the implications of what you're saying. Thinking never engages the present moment. I think we can agree that reality exists only in the present moment. So the inevitable conclusion is that we spend almost no time in reality."

"Wow! I see what you're saying," says Pat. "We live in our heads."

"Exactly, and in our heads we're living unconsciously. The Lion and the Unicorn patterns represent two different models of how we live in our heads. The bottom line is that we're not *living* life, we're *thinking* life."

Angie looks at me and says, "Okay, how do we fix it? I'm ready to live in the 'now.'"

"I'm glad to hear you say that. Ironically, we already live in the 'now.'

Awakening

The mind is a thief that steals our awareness of now. I'll teach you how to spot this thief. Learn his trick and see what he's up to. You'll more fully awaken to 'now' in the process. If you knew that a thief was stealing your belongings every night, what would you do?"

"Stay awake and watch for the thief?" asks Pat.

"Yes, and when you discover the thief, what's the first thing you'd do?"

"I don't know. Call the police? Shoot him. What?"

I smile and say, "The first thing you do is turn on the light. In fact, we all know that thieves don't come in when the lights are on."

Pat and Angie nod. "That's what we're going to do. I'm going to show you how to stay awake and turn on your light. As long as you do that, the thief can never get you again."

"Okay," asks Angie, "so what's to prevent me from giving up, from not doing anything? I mean, if I take what you're saying at face value, then it doesn't matter what I do, so I can do anything I want, right?"

"Yes, logically that would be true. But let's look at it another way. Let's say you've had this great spiritual epiphany," I counter. "Now, are you going to quit your job, leave Pat, and go to Oregon to become a mushroom farmer?"

"I don't understand. What do you mean?"

"Well, you can clearly see that when we give up, there's nothing but peace, right?"

"Yes." Angie has a funny look on her face, like I'm the funny one.

"Okay, so you just give up and move to Oregon to grow mushrooms."

Angie is still looking at me funny. "But I don't want to grow mushrooms."

I nod my head, "Right. And do you want to give up?"

"No, I don't want to do that, either."

"So, Angie, I'm saying that even though you give up the struggle and you let go of your need to make life frantic and not about peace, you're going to do what you're going to do. It would be impossible for me to conceive of you doing anything that would be out of character. Giving up would be out of character for you. So you're going to do what you might expect someone like you would do. That doesn't mean you won't eventually go to Oregon. But it does mean that you'll always behave in a manner consistent with your being."

"I guess that's true. I certainly would never do something I couldn't conceive of."

I look at Pat and Angie and say, "Just remember this: Right action comes from truth. Reaction comes from the conditioned mind. So all we really need to be concerned with is the way we react. This tells us everything we need to know about what keeps us from experiencing the bliss of our true existence."

Angie is looking a little wide eyed as she takes Pat's hand on the way out the door. I suspect she is taking this idea of being in our heads to its logical conclusion. The conclusion has to be that the world is being run by, our families are being raised by, and our lives are being lived by people who are completely up in their heads and never really present. This makes them dangerously insane since they are all responding to something in their heads, which is rarely very pretty or productive, and not to what is right in front of them.

Chapter 6: The Road to Hell is Paved with Preafference: Believing is Seeing

At the level of mind, your experience of life is always filtered through the mind, and governed by the mind. The mind, which is meant to serve you, has become the master, and the real Master is fast asleep.

Leonard Jacobson

Only a generation ago, the closet that housed the secrets of how the brain works was locked up pretty tight. Recently, neuroscientists have kicked the door open and discovered a storehouse of knowledge, some of which is revolutionary. Preafference is one of those gems that had been locked in the closet.

I have made many references to the limbic system. In effect, this is a hurt, fearful, and angry five-year-old who lives in our heads. In addition, I've pointed out that the limbic system is Grand Central Station for emotions and emotional motivation in the brain. At some level, this can all be construed as brain stuff and too heavy to pay attention to. That would be a mistake.

This chapter is going to blow the lid off the secret of how we humans have been stuck, locked out of the Garden of Paradise, since Eve ate the apple. Even so, we will be discussing the brain and I know technical stuff can be daunting to many of us. I will make it as easy as I can to understand in everyday language.

EMOTION IS ESSENTIAL TO ALL INTENTIONAL BEHAVIOR

For years, I've been telling clients that all behavior is driven by emotions. I had an intuitive sense of this truth, and I was using it to make the point that we need to become aware of what these emotions are: the fear of the Unicorn and the shame of the Lion. Lately I've come to realize that the vaunted decision-making apparatus of the brain also serves emotions. In other words, one purpose of every decision is to alter our emotional state.

Now it appears that I have company amongst neuroscientists. An emerging picture of brain dynamics shows that emotion is a property of intentional behavior. What this means is that the limbic system is highly involved in making us act as we do. Furthermore, it means that all actions are emotional, even though we may have our reasons and rationales that *appear* to negate the emotional component.

Science has found that isolating the limbic system, by severing its connections to the brain stem and the hemispheres, causes perception and goal-directed behaviors to cease. Under these conditions, the test animal will perform a few tasks and behaviors, but it won't do anything or go anywhere intentionally (that is, in pursuit of a specific goal).

It turns out that goals are the foundation of intentional action. The goal always includes a change in the emotional state. But obviously a goal itself cannot change our emotional state. This goal to change states is anticipatory. In other words, emotion is linked to the intention to act in the near future. If you have ever seen a cat getting ready to strike at a mouse or bird, this anticipatory stance is easy to spot.

Neuroscientists believe that action emerges from within and is not a reflex, but is directed at some future, which is determined by the person's evaluation of their evolving condition and history. Therefore, emotion is a projection of past states into an anticipated future. To say that the future is nothing more than the past projected is not off the mark. And to say that the remembered past and the imagined future are functions of the limbic system is on target also.

Here comes the big leap. Logically, then, the remembered past and the imagined future are products of the limbic system, or a hurt, fearful, angry five-year-old.

Back to emotional states for a moment. These goals and state changes can occur in less than a second, or over a longer period as a series of adjustments in a series of behaviors that are linked. When action is planned, the brain anticipates the forthcoming emotional state and places the musculoskeletal system in a stance or state of readiness for the anticipated outcome of the action. (As in the cat poised to leap out for a mouse.) This is all based on experience – past emotional experience.

Actually, emotions are experiences. They are feelings that are attached to actions that are geared toward an anticipated future of gain or loss. This might be with respect to a relationship, our livelihood, or our safety. These emotions as experience are linked to perceptions of changing the world to our advantage.

Just as the limbic system places the body into a state of readiness, the limbic system directs this expectancy to the sensory processors in the brain to tell us what to look for. In other words, the limbic system is in charge of perception and tells the rest of the brain what to be looking for. Believing is seeing!

THE MAP OF WHERE YOU ARE

Many neuroscientists are coming to believe that the role of the limbic system has been dramatically underplayed, even misrepresented. When perception is defined not as a sensation but as a form of intentional action, everything can be seen as starting at the limbic system, the heart of goal-directed activities.

This becomes clearer if we look at the role of the Hippocampus, that seahorse-shaped structure that wraps around the ear. The Hippocampus, as stated before, takes current experience and turns it into short term memory. This memory is episodic in that it creates a framework of complex associates in which the memory is happening. The episodic aspect of its function and its memory bank provides a cognitive map of a person's movement in space and time. As you sit and read this, the Hippocampus has mapped your position in the space where you are sitting as well as a frame of reference for the person having the experience. When you move, that position is updated on the map. The time it took to move is experienced as the lapse that every movement requires. That creates the feeling of the linear passage of time inside the brain. This dynamic operation is a prerequisite if past and future states are to be part of intentional action. This is not just a data bank of objects and locations. This "navigator" is an integral part of every experience along with the Amygdala, which provides the emotional content of each moment. Literally, the feeling of where we are, the context, and the story of our lives comes directly from the limbic system.

PERCEPTION

Perception then becomes emotionally charged action that is happening through space and time, and the limbic system is the central interpreter of our experience in the world. As we saw before, the limbic system learns preferred patterns of action. The way science understands how this works is informed by chaos theory. It seems the brain is a chaotic system and our experiences are attractor patterns that bring order to the chaos of brainwaves and information. The more emotional our experience is, the bigger the force field of the attractor pattern. This is especially true during the first few years of life when survival is the only goal. These attractor patterns form emotional basins into which random sensory inputs slide creating meaning in an otherwise meaningless world. The limbic system is understood to shape the attractor landscape, so perception is formed as action is initiated.

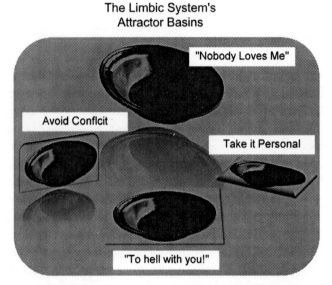

The Limbic System's
Attractor Basins

"Nobody Loves Me"

Avoid Conflcit

Take it Personal

"To hell with you!"

Figure 6-1 The Strange Attractor Landscape of the Limbic System

It's important to note that when the limbic system changes our state, it recruits millions of neuronal nodes in various parts of the brain to cooperate in the new state. These areas of the brain range over broad territory. Researchers believe that vast parts of the brain are recruited into cooperation by the limbic system in the process of perception. This cooperation synchronizes global areas of the neural landscape involved in the state. The result is nothing short of a *hijacking* of the cerebral cortex.

Perception does follow sensory input. However, that which is perceived has been prepared for in advance. The traces of past experience do shape the connections in the sensory cortex. This results in a smoothing of data and a deleting of what might be considered "noise." Experience also biases the cortex toward certain attractor patterns. This enhancement of old patterns conforms to the goals emerging from the limbic system. These perceptions, patterns of meaning-making, and the intentions behind our perception and behavior, have been tuned out and are now ignored because of years of mental repetition. In other words, perception is no longer conscious. We no longer pay attention to that which we are paying attention. The whole machinery runs on autopilot as it slowly pushes us over the edge of a cliff, while we say to ourselves, "I really don't think I like how this is all going."

PREAFFERENCE

So what does *this* six-dollar, multi-syllabic word mean? Let's first look at the meaning of the word afference. It refers to the signaling of nerve cells from external circuits inward toward the central processors of the brain and spinal cord. Afference means incoming information like the information being sent from our eyes to the visual cortex in the brain. Those signals are afferent or moving from the outside in. Preafference, by contrast, means prior to the actual receiving of incoming information. So if seeing visual information was preafferent, we would be making pictures in our heads before the information from the eyes was actually received. If vision were preafferent, we would be constantly stumbling around running into things.

Preafference then refers to the process of *predicting* the consequences of behaviors as an expected inflow of sensory information. Simultaneously, sensory processors in the brain are informed as to the consequence of that behavior and a stance is taken in *anticipation* of that. To say it another way, what you think you see is what you get! Life becomes a series of self-fulfilling prophesies. The conditioned mind sets itself up to reaffirm its conditioning. The road to hell is paved with preafference. Noted brain researcher and theorist, Professor Walter Freeman of the University of California at Berkley, says it this way:

> When a goal directed state emerges . . . with its focus in the limbic system, it contains within it the expectancy of a sequence of sensory inputs. Those anticipated inputs are highly specific to a planned sequence of actions along the way to achieving the specific goal, as well as to a future state of reward, whether it is food, safety, or the feeling of power . . . The organism has some idea of what it is looking for. . . These are Gestalt processes of expectation and attention, which are sustained by motor control and preafference loops. Without preconfiguration, there is no perception. Without sensory feedback, there is no intentional action."

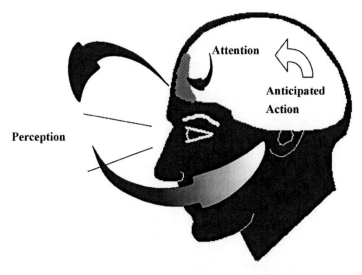

Figure 6-2 The Preafferent Loop

The tail really is wagging the dog! What all of this implies is that we are continually projecting a future from a past and seeing what we think will be there. Until we see what we're doing, our lives become a hopeless repetition of the mistakes of the past. This is especially true of relationships, because they are the crucible of limbic emotional pain that drives nearly all of our behavior. Professor Freeman says the Hippocampus is more like the hub of a wheel than a memory bank or central processor of a computer, and that the limbic system "provides that organization of action with respect to the world." So again, a hurt, angry, fearful five-year-old is at the helm of all intentional behavior. Wow!

PREAFFERENCE IN LIONS AND UNICORNS

Let's look at how this works in relationships. The limbic system of a Lion is organized around shame—that feeling of not being special, not being loved, nobody cares, I'm not important. The limbic system of a Unicorn is organized around fear—fear of abandonment, fear of not making the other happy, fear of failure, fear of things getting out of control, fear of conflict. These form major sources of goal direction for intentional behavior throughout our lives. This is because of the age at which these form during childhood development and our nature or temperament, which provides the initial trajectory for emotional pain formation.

We also know that we need a defense against this pain. Since this is about the survival of the organism (me!), the attractor patterns for the emotional states that buffer the pain are also under the purview of the limbic system. For Lions, the defense-state is anger. For Unicorns, the defense-states are various forms of avoidance and emotional distance as well as resistance and passive-aggressive attacks toward what is perceived to be pressure. Trying to solve the problem of the pain through perfectionism, striving, achievement, workaholism, chronic failure, or a variety of lifestyle-driving emotional states is also located in the limbic nexus. These emotional forces drive our lives. To boil it all down, we operate like the figure below.

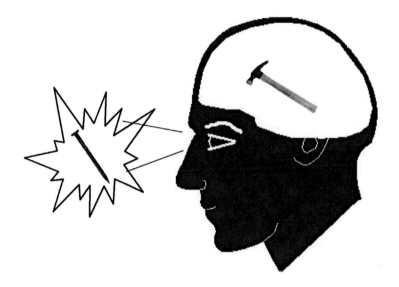

Figure 6-3 If the only tool you have is a hammer, everything looks like a nail.

For Lions, that nail is the expectancy of rejection. For Unicorns, that nail is the expectancy of things being threatening or of being pressured and controlled by another. Our perception drives defenses that carry with them the expectancy of more pain. Counseling professionals will tell you that anxiety, shame, anger, and other negative emotions narrow our focus of attention and fix it on particular aspects of the world. This helps us fulfill the old saying that the definition of insanity is doing the same thing and expecting a different outcome.

Welcome to the human condition! As I'll say over and over, the limbic system is a hurt, fearful, angry five-year-old. This means that preafference nearly guarantees the continuation of that insanity. Or as Peter, Paul, and

Awakening

Mary once sang, *"If I had a hammer, I'd hammer in the morning. I'd hammer in the evening . . ."*

Enough hammering already!

Our world has all of the scars of being beaten with a ball-peen hammer. Clearly this limbic, preafferent, trance that hijacks our lives is not working. There has to be a way out of this loop. That's next.

Chapter 7 Step by Step to Awakening

The ego, e-g-o, the confounded thing that keeps us all imprisoned, the identification No. 1, the cause of all trouble.

Wei Wu Wei

Pat and Angie are sitting in front of me with looks of great expectancy. I've told them we're going to take a big left turn in our work together, and I can see they aren't sure what's going to happen next.

"Okay, are we ready?"

They both nod and I take a deep breath and begin. "In our work in the past, we've primarily focused on your relationship and the issues that come up in your lives together. We've been looking at the Lion/Unicorn theory, and you're really seeing how that operates in your daily lives. I call the level of consciousness you've moved to 'self-observation.' This means that you can see that there are patterns in the limbic system which result in a conditioned mind, and that you are in the grips of those patterns unless you observe the pattern. When you start self-observation, suddenly you see the beginning, middle, and end of the cognitive process."

I walk to my white board and redraw the process diagram that I've used with them many times before. "So perception leads to feelings that are painful and we must defend our pain with some behavior."

Perception ————————➤Feelings ——————➤Behavior

7-1 The Basic Cognitive Process

"Here's what it looks like for Lions and Unicorns," I say as I continue to fill in the diagram.

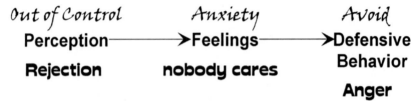

Out of Control   *Anxiety*   *Avoid*

Perception ————————➤**Feelings** ——————➤**Defensive**

Rejection   **nobody cares**   **Behavior**

Anger

7-2 The Cognitive Process for Lions and Unicorns

"For Unicorns the perception tends to be that things are getting out of control, there's going to be conflict, etc. For Lions, the perception is that everything looks like personal rejection. And you see the sequence, which both of you are so familiar with in your relationship and even in the workplace and so on."

Again they nod and I continue. "Now, you are convinced of the existence of these patterns because you can see them. You also know that perception generally is mistaken, and that it comes from that hurt, fearful, angry five-year-old that lives in your heads. Therefore, it all begins with perception. So what we are about to do, if you follow the instructions carefully, will lead to a perceptual awakening."

Pat asks, "You mean we're going to see our relationships differently?"

I smile and say, "Yes, but much more. You'll see everything differently."

"Wow!" exclaims Angie. "That's a pretty big claim. I hope you're right."

"It is and it will happen. I have many clients who have *awakened* and their lives are radically different today. Yours will be, too."

"Okay, I'm ready," says Angie. I notice Pat is a little less enthusiastic. That's a Unicorn's typical fear of the unknown kicking in. Angie, on the other hand, is ready to go "where angels fear to tread" like a typical Lion.

"Very good. Now the reason I say this is going to feel like a left-hand turn is because this doesn't involve discussing your relationships or Lion/Unicorn dynamics, or even early childhood—at least not directly. What I'm going to do is simple, but at first it feels counterintuitive. Don't let that throw you. So get comfortable. Here we go."

Pat and Angie rearrange themselves a bit and try to become less tense.

"What I want you to do is to wait for the next thought that appears in your mind and when it does, focus on it and tell me what happens."

Pat closes his eyes while Angie gets very quiet. Suddenly she looks at me and says, "I don't think I can do this."

"That was the next thought, Angie." I turn to Pat. "What was your experience?"

Pat looks a bit skeptical and says, "I was just thinking that I hope I get the right thought."

I laugh. "Pat, that's so typical of a Unicorn. Can you feel the fear? You're trying to guess what I want so I won't get upset. Do you see where your mind just went?"

He looks at me, and as his eyes grow wide he says, "Oh, my God. I did the same thing with you that I do with Angie. Let's try again."

"Okay, but before we do, I want to do something else to prepare you to do the exercise again. Go inside your mind and silently say, 'My name is Pat,' or 'My name is Angie.'"

I notice that they both do this very rapidly. "Now notice that internal voice. Got that? Also, notice that there's a familiar 'me' feeling that goes with it."

We humans have this very natural process of a voice speaking in our heads on an almost continual basis. For Pat and Angie, this was easy. "Now, that voice you just heard speaking in your head is what you'll be looking for. About 90% of all thought is that voice speaking. We identify it as ourselves, so we never see it as an independent thought-form."

I gesture toward Angie. "For you, the voice said, 'I don't think I can do this.'" Turning to Pat I say, "For you, the voice said, "I hope I get the right thought.'"

"Okay, so let's try again. Wait for the next thought and when you see it, tell me what happens to the thought. In other words, I want you to *observe yourselves experiencing thought*. You'll be shifting to the prefrontal lobes to do this." I gesture toward my forehead. "Okay, ready set go."

I watch as Pat and Angie wait for the next thought. I know this will happen almost instantly. When one is new to the exercise, it seems like a struggle.

Angie turns to me. "I'm not getting this at all." She turns to Pat and asks, "Are you?" Pat shrugs his shoulders.

"I understand. At first, this feels really weird. Just imagine that your mind is like the big white screen at a movie theater. In the theater, we can see and hear things, but we remember that we're in the audience. So any thought-form will appear to us as a picture or a sound. Analogously, then, any movement in mind is defined as thought. Most of the thoughts will be that voice you heard. The voice is speaking all of the time. Primarily, listen to the voice. It's always speaking. The problem is that we never distinguish it as a thought. We think it's 'me,' but it's not me. It's *thought*. So try it again."

Angie starts to laugh.

"What?"

"The voice said, 'This is a dumb exercise.'"

"So you heard it as a thought?"

"Yes, as soon as I became aware of the comment I became aware that I was thinking. It's weird."

Pat, "What was your experience?"

Pat smiles, "I heard the voice, too. In fact, I'm hearing it now. It is always talking. It's as if I'm rehearsing what I'm going to say right now. I can hear it."

"Okay, that's great. So you both have had the experience of observing yourself experiencing thought. So let's do the exercise again. This time, when you become aware that thought is being experienced, look at the thought with your awareness. Scrutinize the thought. Something miraculous is going to happen. I want you to see the miracle before you leave today."

Pat and Angie go to work on another attempt at thought watching.

Angie looks up and says, "It goes away. It just disappears."

Pat nods and says, "The voice just stops. It just stops."

"Okay, I get the exercise, but why is it going to change things in my life?" Angie asks.

"What you're going to learn is that that voice is perception. In other words, if you go back to the diagram and look where it says 'Perception,' we could add the 'voice' right in front of perception since the voice is telling us what everything means." I get up and do that.

The "Voice" Speaks ➤ Perception ➤ Feelings ➤ Defensive Behavior

7-3 The Voice starts the Cognitive Process

Pat gets a grave look on this face. "You mean the voice says something like, 'She's getting out of control,' and then I immediately get anxious and try to avoid?"

Angie looks from Pat to me and says, "You're right. I know you're right. My voice says, 'You'll be rejected,' just before I try to talk to Pat. I just became aware of that. I know it's been going on all of my life with various people. Weird!"

"Of course those are among the most important things the voice says," I offer. "But you will find, as you get used to watching, that the voice is talking all the time about any number of things that occur at random. Let's try again."

Pat and Angie try the exercise a couple times more, and I question them to make sure that everything is working and they understand what their minds are doing.

"Alright, so off you go. I want you to intensely watch your thoughts until we get together next time. You'll find that the easiest time to do it is when you're in your car alone. You have no distractions and no overt pressure. Just watch your mind and learn this skill."

#

"So just watch what your mind does, Jared. There's no trick to it. Just wait for the next thought and tell me what you see." Two weeks ago Jared was a new client, and I decided trying Witness Thought Therapy™ with him (details in Chapter 12). This was my initial treatment plan. Prior to this, I would have gone through the entire Lion/Unicorn theory with him and done a little work with the psychodynamics of his family. In this case, I've decided to start with the skill of "watching" to see if this might be quicker and more effective.

I am beginning to wonder if it was such a good idea. This is our second session. During the first, I relentlessly tried to showing him what it meant to watch his thoughts, but with little success. I'm going to try one more time and shift gears if I am still not having any results. So I tell him again of what thought watching is.

"You know," he says, "this watching reminds me of when I was in graduate school. We used to have to sit in prayer for ten minutes before the first class in the morning. Not that I really minded it, but this exercise reminds me of it." Jared went on for a moment or two reminiscing about graduate school and telling a delightful story about how they were mandated to pray at the Christian school he attended.

"Jared, thanks for sharing that with me. But the purpose of this exercise is to get you to separate yourself from thought, not to identify with it and go off on a tangent."

Jared looks at me a little embarrassed. "I guess I need to pay closer attention, sorry."

I try to think of a good metaphor to explain what we're doing. If I can put it in just the right way, he'll get it and be off to the races. "Think of a thought as a horse with an empty saddle. It wants you to get in the saddle, so it can take you for a ride. Now if you get on the horse, it will take you to the next thought and then to the next. Soon it will be a story and then a drama with pathos and tears, or laughs or whatever. The objective here is just to look. Got it?"

"Got it."

"Ok, Jared, just wait for the next thought. As I said, it will probably be that voice in your head speaking. Look at it and tell me what happens."

Jared looks reflective for a moment and says, "I was just thinking of politics. I have no idea why. I hate politics. I think all politicians should be thrown in jail."

"Jared, Jared!" I try to stop him.

"Huh? What? I didn't do it right?"

"Just notice what you did do. I don't need to hear your opinion about politicians. Don't let the thoughts carry you away. Just look at the thought. If you need to say something about it or if you have an emotional reaction, that means you've identified with the thought instead of watching it."

I think for a minute about how I can make this a little clearer. Then I say, "How about if we try this? I'm going to say a word and you watch your mind. Okay?"

"Okay, shoot."

"Rabbits."

"I see little cotton tails."

"Baseball."

"I hated when they went on strike."

"Jared, do you see the problem? You can't separate yourself from your thoughts at all. Each thought has you by the throat. You think you have to react to each one of them. This isn't a game where you react to each thought. It's a game where you merely watch each thought." I can see that Jared is trying sincerely to understand. At that moment an idea comes to me.

"Jared, how do you know that shirt you are wearing is your shirt?"

He looks down at his shirt and says, "Because I put it on this morning."

"Exactly, so how do you know that voice in your head is your voice?"

I see him deep in introspection then he looks at me with a question in his eyes.

"You know they are your thoughts, that that voice is your voice, because you put it on. You take it on. You give it authority over you. You don't think my shirt is your shirt do you?"

"No, of course not."

"Right, why not?"

"Because it's on you, not me."

"Exactly, the same is true with thought. We only think thought belong to use because we identify them as ours. But what if we didn't identify with them? What if we looked at them like a foreign object?"

Jared reflects for a moment. "I think I see what you are getting at. It's as if the Russians embedded a chip in my head that talks to me and I think it's me, but it's not. It's the Russians giving me instructions. Just like in one of those spy movies."

"Exactly, think of it that way and just sit back and watch how the Russians are programming your brain."

"I think I've got it. Try again."

"The President. . . Congress. . . Dogs . . . Sprinklers"

This time I notice that Jared is intensely concentrating and not commenting when I throw out the random words. Okay, what was your experience?"

"Association! Every word you said, my mind associated it with another word or idea. I tried very hard not to take it on, but only to observe."

"Right, the primitive brain works by association. Since it has to be ready with a survival strategy in any given moment, it's constantly making associations with things from the past, other concepts, ideas – a stream of consciousness that carries us along like a river."

"Okay, doc, I get the point. But what's wrong with letting our thoughts carry us along?"

"As long as we identify with thought, our experience of life is limited to the content of thought."

"Yeeeaah?" Jared looks at me with a confused smile.

"Try this experiment. Imagine you're walking in a forest, and you come upon a tree that catches your eye because it's so beautiful. You stare at it, transfixed. Let me ask you a question. What are you experiencing?"

"The tree?"

"Pretty obvious isn't it? Now continue to imagine that you're taking in the tree and all of a sudden, a thought comes through your mind, 'Hey, that's a beautiful tree.' Now what's your experience?"

Jared looks at me with a suspicious gaze. "It's a trick question isn't it? I'll bite. I'm still experiencing the tree."

"Not correct. You are experiencing your *thought* about the tree. Now your mind is working, comparing, classifying, and associating this tree with other trees you've seen. Believe it or not, you are no longer present with the tree. You are present with your head."

"I'm present with my head. You mean at some level, I'm gone. I'm not there anymore with the tree?"

"You can either attend to your thinking or to your direct experience. You can't be in two places at once. Of course, this describes the mental sickness of humankind. We're stuck in our heads, compulsively thinking. Someone might wonder if we spend so much time in our heads, are we ever really here? Oh, and to answer your question, when you get really good at watching what goes on inside yourself, you'll feel the shift when you leave the present moment and go into your thoughts. So you can either experience 'now' or get lost in thought."

As Jared leaves I feel a sense of satisfaction. He got it finally, and I know it's not easy. At first it's a bit of a mind bender to try and separate from the voice in our heads. But once the concept is understood, it is relatively easy to do. For most of us, it is simply something that would never have occurred to us.

Chapter 8: the Dialogical Self

All voices in your head belong to parts of the ego. The doer who asks, "What shall I do?" and "What do I want?" is the ego.

eli jaxon-bear

THE VOICE IN YOUR HEAD

Somewhere around the age of three, give-or-take, we learned to talk in our head. We created a comfortable imaginary friend called "me" that talks to us inside. It takes up occupancy in a familiar "me" position and speaks from that podium for the rest of our lives.

We have imaginary conversations with others and ourselves. Most of the time we're talking to an unseen listener parked somewhere in the recesses of gray matter between our ears. The talking goes on and on. Our fascination with our "selves" grows to the point where we never let up or shut up. We become so addicted to the voice in our head that after so many years we don't pay any attention to it. This is a mistake of biblical proportions.

Imagine if you will that when you were about three years old, someone gave you a toy. But this was no ordinary toy. This was a marvelous toy. It was put into your hands, and over the course of months you were given complete training in how to use this unbelievable device. Let's put it in modern technological terms. Let's say it was a cell phone, PDA, video game, stereo, and home theater all rolled into one.

For those of you who are not consumer electronics wonks, this analogy probably won't mean much. But you know how so many of us love our electronics. So go with this example for a bit if you will.

We all know of a teenager who won't come out of his room because he's addicted to video or computer games. Maybe you're addicted to high-definition TV and home theater with surround sound. Possibly, you have one of those combination cell phone, PDA, and mp3 players all rolled into one. Okay, you get the picture.

So what if we put that all in the hands of a three-year-old and progressively taught him or her how to use that technology, all the features, and gave the child upgrades as they became available? It probably wouldn't take too long before you had someone hopelessly addicted to their toy. If we were to fast forward the clock to the person's fortieth birthday, we would probably find them helplessly surfing the Web for the latest gadget. This describes our fascination and addiction to the voice in our heads!

THE PREAFFERENT "ME"

As we humans take intentional action through space-time, the limbic system emotes, maps, and predicts the consequences of our actions. As we saw earlier, the limbic system is, according to many scientists and theorists, the organ of volition in us. With the hurt, fearful, angry five-year-old at its helm, the brain is an anticipatory system constantly responding to an imaginary future. All the while this happens, the internal "me" is preparing for what to say next.

Every time we make a new association with the external or internal environment, part of our anticipatory process is thinking about what to say next. In fact, we say it! In our heads! If you pay close attention to the voice in your head, you'll find that it's normally doing one of two things. Either it's regurgitating a past conversation or it's rehearsing a future conversation. Most of the time it's the latter. The voice fills our head with what we expect to say—often just as soon as the person we're with has finished their sentence—which means that, as we rehearse, we aren't listening to them.

Of course, we don't have to be in conversation with another person. The head of the passive motorist on his or her way to work is a veritable cacophony of possibilities: what to say to the boss, how to argue a point with a customer, and Get your SUV outta my way!

The preafferent "me" certainly is the "dialogical self." But whether this is dialogue or monologue is hard to pin down. Perhaps dialogue is a better way to think of it, as it usually involves a "me" talking to a "you." This "you" rarely responds. More often, "you" is in rapt attention to the pearls of wisdom cascading from "me." Even as I write these words, I'm talking to an imaginary you, a you who is cordial and highly impressed with all that I'm saying. Yes, my head is dialoguing these words in my internal voice as I type into my computer. Perhaps this is one of the more legitimate uses of the dialogical self.

Theorists disagree amongst themselves about the arrangement of characters and their positions in our heads. Furthermore, they continue to discuss how dialogical relationships are created and maintained. Some think there is a variety of positions that house different characters as they emerge in our heads. Some think that each voice appears in a serial fashion, while others believe the process moves in parallel.

All one has to do to resolve the most critical issue is to say your name silently in your head. The "me" takes up occupancy in a familiar "I" position that is undeniable. Regardless of any other theory, that "me" that is constantly speaking is where all the trouble for humankind begins. Again, the critical idea that theorists express is that the dialogical self has a distinct purpose. Its purpose is to prepare each of us for encounters in the immediate future. The voice anticipates the next moment and it is saying something about it.

Here is where that preafferent, dialogical self comes full circle. All of this is right in line with the discussion of the preafference of the limbic system. It seems logical to conclude that the same preafferent loop that encircles perception and intentional action also includes our internal voice commenting on the immediate future as we go along.

Theorists also speculate that the dialogical self is ego-centred and concerned with social interactions. This seems reasonable since most of the internal dialogue has to do with intended, rehearsed, or regurgitated speech involving another person, real or imagined.

PERCEPTION REVISITED

Earlier the point was made that without preconfiguration there is no perception. What this means is that the limbic system tells our senses and the sensory processors in the brain what to expect next. Now we have to include the voice in our heads, the dialogical self, as part of that preconfiguration. The implication of this is overwhelming.

Let me explain by telling a story of what happened in a recent workshop. There was a woman—call her Gloria. We were working together on a process. I can't remember too well what the process was exactly, but I vividly remember what happened next. I instructed her to listen to the voice in her head before she shared the next step in the process.

She looked at me with a surprised look on her face and said, "The voice just said, 'I'm going to be rejected.'"

In that moment, all kinds of realizations came cascading into her mind. Of course, the voice had been saying the same thing virtually all of her life, but she had become so used to it that she no longer even noticed it. My directing her attention inward broke the spell of silence. There was the voice telling her in no uncertain terms what was happening before it happened. So before she shared with the group, she had the preconception that the group would reject her.

But the epiphany didn't stop there. A piece of the insight was how personal rejection had driven her marriages to fail. In addition, she worked with disadvantaged children. What better place to re-enact her issues around rejection and struggle to resolve them, than to work with outcast children? Clearly she was projecting herself into the children and vicariously working out her struggle with rejection. All this came to her in a flash.

The next day when I saw her, her feet still hadn't touched the ground and the integration of this new information was still continuing. This voice, driven by her limbic emotional pain that had been out of her awareness, had suddenly been caught red-handed. Her life would never be quite the same, and her level of consciousness had indeed been raised a level.

Sadly in that same workshop sat Teresa. She never could distinguish the voice in her head, but continually responded with philosophy and opinions. She talked about the drama of her life story. This monologue was nothing more than a regurgitation word for word of what the voice in her head was saying. Nothing I could say or do, including drawing diagrams or showing examples would penetrate the stranglehold of identification with her thinking.

Another example of this preconfiguration of perception occurred just the other day, a client told me of a dilemma she was experiencing. Her stepdaughter was graduating from middle school the same day that her nephew, her brother's son, was playing in a championship baseball game. She couldn't decide which event to attend. As a result, her husband was going crazy. He couldn't understand how the nephew could be nearly as important as the stepdaughter.

I instructed her to listen to any voice she might hear in her head when I gave her a signal. I said to her, "You need to choose between the two. Imagine choosing and watch for a voice in your head."

She looked at me in surprise and said, "I hear my mother's voice saying, 'Don't let me down!'" She explained that her mother turned every special event and holiday into a *forced march* for the family, and if a family member didn't meet her expectations, she would load tons of guilt on them. In essence, what was happening was that every time she tried to decide which choice was correct, the voice in her head would bring her up short, and she would become paralyzed with guilt.

The irony of the whole thing was that her brother had known of the conflict in the schedule and told her that her presence at the baseball game was certainly optional and not to worry about it! Once we worked it through, she felt the fetters lift and reassured her husband that there was no longer a question of supporting his daughter.

The point behind this discussion is that our internal dialogue is what gives our perception its meaning, especially in the social arena. At the end of the process are, of course, our defenses. This means that the anger of the Lion and the avoidance and resistance of the Unicorn are direct responses to the unacknowledged voice. The voice in the head of the Lion is saying words to the effect of, "You are being rejected" while the voice of the Unicorn is in effect saying, "This is going to get out of control." Of course, there are individual variants of this, but I believe that the repertoire of voice/ perceptions that drive our basic defensive system is limited to only two or three phrases. Of course, the voice talks all the time about everything; but when it comes to our personal pain, the rhetoric is somewhat limited. This serves to narrow our focus of attention, and the preafferent self-fulfilling prophesy continues.

WHENCE COMES THE VOICE?

This gets a little tricky, as the limbic system itself does not control speech. However, theorists feel that the dialogical self emerges in the neural circuits where attention and intentional action come together. This describes the network that connects the limbic system and the prefrontal lobes.

Remember from our previous discussion that goal-directedness tends to come from the limbic system. The prefrontal lobes' sole contribution to the voice in our heads would be focusing our attention on that which the voice is directing, *rejection* for instance. This is perception, pure and simple. The voice directs perception. The prefrontal lobes scan for what they expect to be there.

Concentrated bundles of nerve fibers connect the limbic system, specifically the Amygdala, to the prefrontal lobes and back again. This interconnection allows the activation of these two areas simultaneously and mutually. Emotional signals move toward the forehead to direct focus and attention while attention regulates emotion in a downstream path to the limbic system.

The problem with this arrangement is that the upstream path from the Amygdala to the prefrontal area is a stronger and quicker connection than the regulating pathway leading in the other direction. That's why so many of us struggle with our emotions getting out of control. The prefrontal lobes cannot always inhibit the emotional impulses so many of us have problems with anger, anxiety, and so many of our primitive reactions.

When we talk to ourselves, this interconnection and resulting reciprocal interaction between the prefrontal and limbic areas produces a coupling that results in a synchronized attentional state. Meanwhile, massive recruitment takes place initiated by the limbic system that involves the rest of the cortex and more primitive parts of the brain. The state becomes global and the voice speaks from a familiar "I" position inside the head. Attached to this voice comes an equally familiar feeling of "me." This produces a "subjective" state of "me" experiencing the "objective world." In other words when we talk to ourselves we create a subjective "me" experiencing an *object* which is the focus of our attention. This *object* could be any *thing* like an internal representation of another person or an external picture of the scene right in front of us.

The voice has interesting characteristics. It sounds like us. It feels like us. It has the same tone and timbre as our own voice. How is it, then, that the voice is so familiar over the years? Clearly, it feels like the same voice I had when I was a teenager; but certainly, the characteristics of it have changed with the years. Possibly, that familiarity is only an illusion that comes with the feeling of "me" housed in that familiar "I" position. Finally, it is sublingual. If you pay attention to the voice and its activation characteristics, you will find that it tickles the tongue. It feels like a sub-vocalization that would leap out of your mouth at an inopportune time.

In fact, close observation of the voice reveals that in times of stress with another person, it is literally feeding you dialogue or the lines to say to the other person. It is as if an understudy, standing off stage somewhere nearby, feeds us the lines that we speak.

Even though we spend most of our time in the subjective "me" state talking to an imagined listener or ourselves, we are able to conjure up the essence of or a gist-like representation of nearly anyone to whom we might want to talk. Mothers, fathers, wives, bosses—all swirl around that internal voice as we rework failed conversations, re-experience our own eloquence, or rehearse imaginary conversations designed to straighten out the other person represented in our head. We are always ready with something pithy to say to the predictable, but imaginary response of another.

These dialogues go on by themselves totally unattended. As previously stated, they go on to the point that we no longer pay any attention. As our internal state shifts with anticipated perception, our voice is instantly ready, talking to us about a topic that's associated with that state change. If there is nothing to associate with, the voice merely speaks at random. The brain ensures that we are never at a loss for words.

At least we have that going for us.

Chapter 9: The Identified Thinker

. . . it can be said that the ego is a compilation of positionalities held together by vanity and fear. It is undone by radical humility which undermines its propagation.

David Hawkins

"I notice that when I watch the thoughts and they disappear, I'm so much more at peace," Angie comments as we start our session.

Pat says, "Yeah, it's the peace alright. Doc, you done good. You helped me get back to the peace."

Pat's statement has a tone of finality to it. I hope that's not true. So many people, including some of my clients, have convinced themselves that they've gotten it. More precisely their ego-mind has convinced them that they have it, and then they go right back into the madness of thought-identification. This is especially dangerous to someone who has had a legitimate awakening experience of some kind. That kind of experience leads directly to spiritual insight, and the ego can grab ahold of it. The ego then puts on the cloth of this spiritual knowing like an overcoat. When the ego becomes "spiritual," the person goes back into their mind without knowing it and gets lost.

"Pat, you make it sound like the journey of discovery is over for you."

Pat shrugs his shoulders. "In a way, I guess I am saying that. I mean, I know that as long as I watch my thoughts I'll be in peace. So what's the problem?"

I lean forward and say, "The problem is that what you have discovered is a *path*, not a *destination*. If you choose to continue on down the path, there is much work to be done. If you stop and assume you've made it, you become subject to the constant attack of the ego-mind. You have found a way to displace it, but it won't be satisfied to let you have your life back."

I realize as I am talking to Pat that I am making the ego-mind out to be the enemy. If fact it is nothing more than our identification with the activity of the brain and nervous system. It is far more a tool than the enemy. But I will often paint the situation like this to motivate the person to become the master instead of the slave.

Angie looks perplexed. "If I'm hearing you correctly, it's like we now have a tool. Now we have to learn to use it?"

"Yes, there's much more of the mind to explore, and the ego has many tricks it will play with you to get you back to being its servant. For now, it's been caught red-handed. It's like a little boy who's been helping himself to the cookie jar. Finally, you've poked your head around the corner and it jerked its hand back."

"It's funny you should mention that. That's real close to the feeling I get." Pat runs his hand through his hair. "For me, it's like discovering a thief in the house. It's as if I've been trying to catch the thief without ever turning on the light. Now I know how to turn on the light."

Angie pipes up and says, "I just tell the thoughts to go away. Then I try to replace them with better thoughts. That voice inside my head is a trash talker. It's always judging everyone else, putting them down. It's not a pretty place in there."

"Angie," I reply, "you bring up a couple of interesting points. I've noticed there's an important developmental phase that everyone seems to go through when they start witnessing their thoughts. At first, we're horrified at what we see. The ego-mind is a place of violence, hostility, and arrogance. So our natural reaction is to try to either suppress the thoughts or replace them with better thoughts. Let me add one more point about this. Lions find their thoughts to lean heavily toward the hostile and retaliatory, while Unicorns tend to spend a lot of time anticipating, planning, constructing scenarios and so forth. I had one clients call it 'stacking boxes.' His internal voice and mental activity were devoted to getting everything just so, in the right order, and in the right place"

"What's wrong with corrective action?" asks Pat. "Seems like the right thing to do to me."

I smile and say, "Yes, I agree. But it's like the thief you mentioned has now dressed up like a police officer to help you catch the thief. The thoughts to suppress thought or to replace one thought with a better thought come from the same ego-source as the original thought. At first, we need to go through this stage where it seems like we need to take pretty dramatic action, since the mind is not a nice place. But you soon realize that the *watching itself is the transformation.*"

Angie says, "I see what you mean, but it's hard not to want to do something about the thoughts. Mine are so violent and judgmental. That voice seems to hate everyone and everything. How did we get into this mess?"

I walk to the white board and start drawing a picture of the brain with the limbic system and the prefrontal lobes. "Now the voice in our heads appears as a function of a coupling of the limbic system with the prefrontals. The limbic system provides our orientation in time, space, and emotion. The prefrontals provide the attention. My picture looks like this:

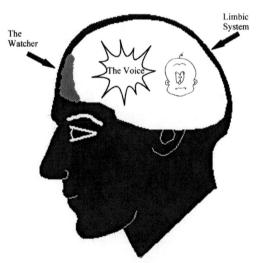

Figure 9-1 The *voice* emerges.

"Now remember that the voice begins to emerge when we're old enough to start talking. Also, remember that the limbic system is pretty much completely developed by the time we're five. There's still some development that takes place in the Hippocampus, but the attractor patterns for our emotional woundedness have certainly been established by our early interactions with our parents. The prefrontal lobes are underdeveloped at this point.

"My theory is that the watcher, the prefrontals, thinks that the voice is a function of itself since those lobes get wired so much later than the limbic system. What I'm trying to say is that since the voice has almost always been there, we just assume that it's *us*. The watcher is fooled into thinking that the voice belongs to it. So we *identify* with the voice, go along with whatever it says, and learn to ignore it since it feels so familiar."

Pat looks at Angie and then turns to me. "We are not our thoughts, are we?"

"We are not our thoughts, no. We are not even the *thinker* of the thoughts unless we choose to think. When thinking happens automatically, it is being generated through association by the self-preserving parts of the brain. If you study the motives of thought, you'll find they are always *self-enhancing*. The limbic system wants the personality to survive at everyone else's expense."

Angie asks, "How can you say that we aren't the *thinker* of the thoughts? They come from us, don't they?"

"Angie, look right now at the mind. You now know how to look, correct?" Angie nods.

"Okay, look at thought." Angie turns introspective. I notice Pat is doing it along with her. "Now, are you your thoughts?" They both shake their heads. "Are the thoughts coming from you?"

Angie looks up and says, "No, but how can that be?"

I say, "Look at your foot. Are you the foot?"

"Oh, I get it," says Pat. "It's like we've been going around all of our lives thinking we were the foot. Everything the foot did, we identified with. We told our friends we were the foot. We believed we were the foot."

"Exactly. We believe we are the *thinker*. It feels like us. It's been there virtually all of our lives. It sounds like us. It even has the timbre of our own voice. There's one more thing that makes the identification even more complete. There's this 'me' feeling that goes with the whole thinking process. So it all must be 'me.'"

"Okay, okay, then here's a question," states Angie. "If I'm not my thoughts, then who am I?"

"Remember when we were talking about the prefrontal lobes? What quality do they have? What is their main function, at least from the perspective of our conversation?"

"Watching?" Pat ventures a guess.

"Yes, or put another way, the presence of awareness, our sense of being. So what we are is awareness watching the thinker."

Angie sits back and muses, "I am awareness."

"Prove this to yourself. Watch your thoughts and realize this truth; *awareness can know thought, but thought can never know awareness.*"

#

Rebecca is an evangelical Christian. I love working with evangelicals, since I get to quote scripture to them. My less religious clients get a little nervous when I refer to the Bible, because so much of what has been associated with those scriptures is negative in their minds.

"I'm telling you he disgusts me. Pornography is of the devil." Rebecca has a huge issue with her husband's habit of downloading sexual images from the Internet. But she has an even bigger issue seeing her own seething need to retaliate instead of accept and forgive. I know my chances of making progress with this type of person are slim at best. But I can't allow myself to struggle with success or failure. I just need to stay present.

"It's morally wrong. It's against everything the Bible and the blood of Christ stands for. The scripture specifically prohibits the lust of the flesh," she continues.

We have been going around and around for several sessions. I wonder if I will ever be able to break her out of the drama that grips her. "Rebecca, you love the Lord with all your heart, don't you?" I ask in a comforting voice.

Rebecca's eyes fill with tears and she says, "Yes, more than anything. I do."

I know that this isn't real love; it is the need to be seen as being *good*. This is left over from something she learned to survive in her family of origin. She doesn't see that though. It is a trance state from her limbic system that has hijacked her completely. But the frightened child within her firmly believes that if she does everything according to the rules, and colors inside of the lines that she won't be abandoned. I have seen this pattern many times before. Rebecca's problem is that she doesn't see that her drive for religious practice is a survival strategy that is polluting her genuine yearning for spiritual fulfillment.

In our previous sessions I have tried to get her to see her part, to look at herself, but my many attempts have failed. She is lost in judgment, the judgment she has against her husband. She doesn't see that judgment as a form of violence full of attack thoughts.

Today a new approach has occurred to me that just might be what changes this log-jam. Now it's my turn to speak.

"Rebecca, I'm confused about something."

Rebecca looks up at me as if to say, 'What could be confusing about that?'

"Isn't disgust a form of hate?" I know I am laying a trap for her. I know

I risk offending her, but people who are so convinced they are right don't tend to respond to anything subtle.

Rebecca mumbles, "I suppose so."

"And doesn't the Apostle John say that if someone says he loves God but hates his brother he is a liar and a murderer, and that a murderer has no eternal life in him?" (1 John 3:15, 4:20)

Rebecca looks at me as a number of emotions sweep across her face. The first looks like a bit of anger and disagreement. Then her eyes grow wide with recognition. I wonder if that means she sees her own hypocrisy. Finally, she bursts into sobs of what appear to be repentance. Hopefully, she sees what she has done – the hate filled thoughts, the judgment, the violence, and darkness of the mind.

I sit still and settle into the absolute silence that surrounds her sorrow. A few minutes and many tissues later, she finally gathers herself to reply to me. "You have told me to watch my thoughts. You have told me of that voice in my head. I guess I should have listened."

"Rebecca, imagine Paul. He's on his way to Damascus and he has an *awakening* (Acts 9:8). Because of this, he talks about how we are corrupted by the impulses of the flesh and the dark imaginings of the mind. He says we mind the things of the flesh. Don't you see? Both you and your husband are trapped in the mind."

Rebecca is still shaken by what she had seen about herself. "I just thought if I was *good* that. . ." Her voice trails off.

"It's not about good or bad. It's about life or death. Doesn't Paul say to be transformed by the renewing of your *mind*? He doesn't say to be transformed by acting like the 'good' one in the relationship. He says that if you are carnally minded you're dead (Romans 8:6). In many translations, it's called 'the mind of the flesh.' Do you know what that means?"

"Obviously, I don't."

"It means the mind of thought-identification, a mind where thought has the authority over the person. This leads to drama, fascination, positions, and philosophies. Can you imagine going to the pearly gates and having God ask for your opinion about something? 'So Rebecca, tell me what you think about your husband's pornography'—like that's ever going to happen. No, we have our hands full with one person. It's the person wearing our shoes. Our ego longs for those things that give us delight. This usually comes at someone else's expense."

Rebecca looks at me and I can see now she is fully present.

"But, but," she stammers.

That 'but' means she has recovered, her ego is back in charge, and she wants to argue the scripture. Here we go.

"Paul says we need to mortify the flesh (Romans 8:13). If it doesn't mean dirty sexual things, what does it mean?" She says as if to challenge me.

"It means our *arrogance,* not our genitals. He says we have weapons that demolish strongholds and pretenses (2 Corinthians 10:4-5). The greatest pretense of all is that *we think we know something,* and we're going to tell the world what we know. And we're going to punish people we think are wrong. We go around bashing and judging."

"Okay, but what are our weapons supposed to be?"

"Rebecca, you're assuming that the battlefield is *out there* somewhere, amongst the great masses of nonbelievers. The battlefield is your mind. That's where the strongholds are. The problem is your ego, your spiritual pride, and the fact that you think you're better than anyone. The stench of arrogance and judgment is the disobedience that Paul is talking about. His remedy? Hold captive every thought to make thought obedient (2 Corinthians 10:5). All our lives, *thought* is the master. We make it obedient by holding it captive."

"I see what you mean. I never thought of it that way. I guess I've got a lot to learn."

"The problem has been our understanding of the scripture. We think Paul is talking about the lust of the flesh as some morality theme. He means the greedy longings of the mind. Our expectations, our insistence that the perfection of the Divine expression of Now be something *we* think it ought to be instead of what it is. We want the assurance of our own resources as the answer to all. The promise of future fulfillment is the trick of the ego."

Rebecca recoils visibly at the thought that she might just have to accept what is. "But the world is evil. We have to work to make it better. Don't we?"

"Do we? Look, Rebecca, what are the characteristics of God? You know, those qualities that everyone agrees belong to God and God alone?"

Rebecca thinks for a minute. I can see her mulling over the possibilities. Suddenly her eyes light up. "Omniscience, omnipotence, and omnipresence," she states with conviction.

"Correct! Now think about the real meaning of omnipresence for a moment. What does that really mean?"

"God is always present. He is always here. He is everywhere."

"Rebecca, 'omni' means infinite. It means that God is infinitely present. It doesn't mean God is present here *in* this room. It means that God *is* the room. The chair is God. You are God. If God is infinitely present, then there is nothing but God. That being the case, we're going to judge that 'what is' is unacceptable? 'What is' is God and only God. We like to say that everything is God. No, God is everything."

Rebecca looks at me as if I'm a bit crazy until the force of my point finally dawns on her. "You're right. It has to be the case. I must confess that I never saw it from that point of view."

"Paul says we see 'through a glass darkly' (1 Corinthians 13:12), which is a really awkward way of saying we see through a dark glass. Our perception is clouded and distorted by the conditioned mind, our lower nature, the carnal mind. We want to judge for ourselves what's good and evil, what's blessing and misfortune. We want to be God's God."

"So what do I do? If I am that deeply trapped what do I do?"

"Watch your thoughts. Watch that voice. You know, I say 'watch the voice' and that sounds a little weird. But for me it's an easier way to describe the awareness than simply listening to the voice."

Rebecca looks reflective and says, "How will my life be different? If I watch, I mean."

"Remember the exercise we did where you forgot everything?" I ask her. "Remember the peace?"

"Yes."

"When we become the 'identified thinker,' we lose the peace. When we give up, surrender, and look with innocent perception, the peace emerges from within us. The identified thinker is hopelessly lost in the drama of this world, the world of the flesh. We have given thought complete authority over us. Then we are lost. We have no life. Life is not found in the world of thought."

I watch Rebecca leave as I've watched so many others leave. Pain brings them in and freedom from pain gives them the excuse to stop the work of being free. I hope that Rebecca isn't one of those. So often when that peace is experienced, people stop the work of growing before they fully catch fire. Eventually they slip back into the madness of thought-identification without even noticing that it has happened.

People want support to end their suffering; but once they feel better, they enter back into the world of drama. Once again, the suffering becomes unbearable.

Chapter 10: Ego-Mind, Conditioned Mind, Mosaic Mind

The mind is restless, unsteady, turbulent, wild, stubborn; truly,
it seems to me as hard to master as the wind.

Bhagavad Gita

We know from psychology that the mind/brain divides itself up into personalities under extreme pressure. There is a psychological disorder called Disassociative Identity Disorder (DID) that used to go under the name of Multiple Personality Disorder (MPD). I raise this topic only to prove that we humans have the ability to form separate personalities on the fly during a certain developmental period of our lives.

The question arises, what's the difference between someone with DID and all of us normals? Well, not much. Really, the only difference between someone with DID and a normal person is that with DID the personalities are often greater in number and are usually completely disconnected from one another. After a disassociative episode, a person with DID very often cannot remember the intrusion of one of the other personalities. We, on the other hand, remain relatively lucid during these transitions.

My intent is not to get into the details of what creates DID. Suffice to say that it is caused by repeated childhood episodes of abuse during which the child thinks they will die. Now not all children in the same situation will develop DID, but the majority will while the rest will develop other psychological problems. These occur concurrent with the dramatic development of the limbic system during the ages of about two to five years old. After about seven years of age, abuse does not result in DID. Abuse that starts later results in a spectrum of symptoms more accurately defined as Acute Stress Disorder or Post Traumatic Stress Disorder.

So what are the purposes of these split-off personalities in someone with DID? Survival and protection. The parts of these people develop in response to the threat of death to protect the person from physical and emotional pain in one way or another.

This extreme condition is only a more dramatic example of what happens to all of us. During those formative years when the limbic system is developing at a furious pace, we all develop personalities to deal with pain and our need to protect ourselves from it.

THE SUB-PERSONALITIES OF THE LION AND THE UNICORN

I use the term "sub-personalities" to denote parts of us that we create and split off in order to protect ourselves from the pain that occurs in those early first relationships in life. As you'll see later, the use of the prefix "sub" is misplaced. But for now it serves the purpose of showing how emotional pain leads to adaptive emotional states that are not a permanent personality, but function only for the purposes of carrying pain and protecting or defending pain.

Let me also put this in the context of the earlier discussion about goal-directed behavior that is spurred by the limbic system. Remember that the brain is a chaotic system and that the emotional states form attractor patterns that serve to help organize intentions and behaviors. A sub-personality or "part" might be conceived as a group of these attractors that are the organizing networks behind a spectrum of associated behaviors, beliefs, attitudes, and expected outcomes or perceptions. An example is a *part* of us that gets angry over perceived rejection or a *part* of us that tries to avoid conflict.

Okay, what are the parts or sub-personalities of the Lion and the Unicorn? We can refer to the modified cognitive model to help us understand.

Figure 10-1 Modified Cognitive Model

First, we all need a personality that carries the pain of our unmet emotional needs. Some of us have more than one part that serves this function. But for Lions, this is definitely the part that carries the pain of rejection—that "nobody cares" pain. For Unicorns, it's the pain of fear. This might be fear of abandonment, or any number of other fears. These would all be subject to the family system and the close interaction with that parent who served the role of the first social relationship.

We all need a defense against pain. This leads to the creation of defensive sub-personalities, which come out to extinguish the pain. For Unicorns, this part tries to avoid conflict. For Lions, this is the angry part.

Finally, we all form sub-personalities that try to solve the problem of the pain through striving. Many of us have parts that are over-achievers, workaholics, perfectionists, pleasers, and the list goes on and on.

As we survey or scan the environment around us, our sensory lenses filter and sort for matches to the triggers for our various parts. We shift from one emotional state to another, sometimes in mid-sentence.

A sub-personality can be seen as a fully functional unit that includes a goal, an emotion, a behavior, and an anticipated perception that converge simultaneously. These states can exist for short durations or operate in the background for extended periods. They define the trajectory of our lives, our careers, and our relationships.

No doubt, each one of these states comes with its own well-rehearsed script for the "voice" in our heads. The *hurt* voice, the *angry* voice, the *philosophical* voice are all tied to these units. To put this in more common vernacular, each goal-directed state is an *act*. Love it or hate it, we all have an act. Life changes dramatically only after a person gets tired of their act.

INTROJECTS AND OTHER VOICES

Another aspect of the ego-mind is introjects. We mentioned this concept earlier. An introject is a mental representation of another person. This is nearly always a mother or father. More specifically, it's the *voice* of mother or father. This disembodied parent who lives in our heads knows exactly when to chime in on cue to warn us when we're overeating, failing, or going to be rejected. Introjects love to issue criticism of a specific kind. In some kinds of therapy, this is known as the "Top Dog," which is the critical voice in our heads. Likely as not, it is an introject. We can always count on mom or dad to be there, interjecting wisdom to change the course of our behavior to make it even more robotic and unconscious than normal. This occurs, of course, even long after they have passed from this plane of existence.

Awakening

We also know how to create an imaginary audience for ourselves in any situation for any purpose. The dialogue that ensues from this has been discussed earlier. We can conjure up the gist of or essence of just about anyone real or imagined and carry on an animated conversation with him or her. This is usually of a preparatory nature. The mind anticipates the next good or bad thing and starts rehearsing immediately.

Let me give an example of something that happened to me this last week. I was coming back from the gym at about 7:00 a.m., when I came to a stop behind another car at an intersection. The place where I stopped put me under a freeway overpass. At that time in the morning, the dim light under the overpass was such that my headlights came on automatically. When that happened, I noticed the face of the driver in front of me in her driver's side mirror. I immediately heard the voice in my head say something to the effect that she might be irritated by my headlights. The next thing I knew, I was having a lively chat with her in my head explaining how my headlights were tied to a light sensor and that I had no control over them coming on due to the dim light under the freeway above me. I was all prepared in the preposterous event that she leapt from her car and accosted me. Had I not been watching my mind, I would have unconsciously prepared my entire physiology for a negative encounter with this other person.

Our own voice added to introjects, sub-personalities, and the voices of real or imagined people all talking in our head creates a cacophony of immense proportions. It pulls us away from the present moment, prepares us for events that never take place, and deceives us that things that never existed are out there somewhere. James H. Austin, M.D., describes it this way in his book, *Zen and the Brain*:

> . . . *thinking is an agitated, Brownian motion of proliferating abstractions and associations. Each sets off a chain reaction. This incessant chatter of thought swirls around the axis of self/other concerns. It leaves little spare time for completely clear, calm reasoning.*

THE CONDITIONED MIND

Conditioning is the cornerstone of how the primitive survival system works. Another word for conditioning is learning. But conditioning carries with it the aspect of brain-washing. Our early learning conditions us to expect things to be a certain way. The brain is designed to function automatically without our having to put in any real effort. Our automatic responses, our introjects, the various voices in our heads, and our sub-personalities form attractor basins within the chaos of neurons and brain waves such that we needn't be conscious of anything.

But conditioning leads to some unexpected consequences. We see things the same way we always did. Our basic emotional responses never really change. We don't ever like things the way they are, at least not for very long. And we keep trying to change the situation we're in by doing the same thing, with nauseating repetition, expecting a different outcome. Unconscious living directed by the conditioned mind leads to human misery. You'd think there would be a powerful incentive for people to snap out of it. But generations have been unconscious. The momentum of unconsciousness and conditioning is an enormous tidal wave that has carried humanity for thousands of years. Sharp and sustained pain is the only thing that ever makes us question our conditioning.

What was originally a survival mechanism driven by biological necessity has run amok. Humanity is profoundly unconscious. The mind of humankind thinks compulsively and automatically without instruction or supervision. We believe every thought, take it on, and let it have authority over us without question. That leads to the next conditioned thought, which leads to the next. Soon we are in the story that conditioned thought is telling, and then we're immersed in the drama of conditioned thought. We then react without thinking.

Then we take all this toxicity and dump it into the heads of our children, so they might become conditioned as we were. This is called *Original Sin*. We are like gods; judging each moment as acceptable or unacceptable. Conditioning makes us dangerously insane. We are unconscious, on autopilot. Despite that, we think we know. We know better, we think we're better-than.

Ego-mind

This leads us to a thing called the "ego." It has been identified as the "ego-mind," the "egoic mind." The Apostle Paul called it the "old man" (Ephesians 4:22), the "carnal mind" (Romans 8:7), the "mind of the flesh" (Romans 8:5). The ego is synonymous with the "self." The self is who we think we are on the inside, while the "personality" is who others think we are. The origin of this from a biological viewpoint is the limbic system. The limbic system is that hurt, angry, fearful five-year-old at the hub of intentional behavior. The personality or self is a bloated generalization of that little kid. It's the child brain metastasized into a dangerously self-centered machine bent on survival at everyone else's expense. All thought, that which the "voice" speaks, is self-enhancing. It is the source of spiritual death. Above all, it wants to be God, and it wants to survive death.

The ego-mind is organized around emotional pain. It doesn't want to feel it. It doesn't want to see it. It wants to deny it. It will do anything to make it go away. In doing so, it worships it. Pain creates the *idolatry* of the ego-mind. Oh, we don't idolize pain. We worship our efforts at not feeling it. There is no acceptance of life just as it is. The ego is the center of resistance, passive or active. It is the master we serve even when we're convinced we're spiritual. It carries with it the most insidious lie of all – the promise of future fulfillment.

In his masterful account of spiritual growth, *A Path with Heart*, Jack Kornfield says that after years of Zen meditation and training in monasteries in Thailand, India, and Sri Lanka:

> *I was still emotionally immature, acting out the same painful patterns of blame and fear, acceptance and rejection that I had before my Buddhist training . . . I had used the strength of my mind in meditation to suppress painful feelings, and all too often I didn't even recognize that I was angry, sad, grieving, or frustrated until a long time later.*

How did Kornfield discover the truth underneath years of spiritual practice? When he came back to the United States after years in the isolation of monasteries, he rediscovered this thing called a *relationship*. Relationships reveal the deepest trance of the ego-mind. Anything left in the shadows comes out to haunt us. The more intimate and committed the relationship is, the deeper the trance and the more powerful the emotional forces we must look at.

The other truth in what Kornfield discovered is that you can't practice your way out of the mind. It is probable that through rigorous spiritual practice many experiences of bliss and mental exaltation can take place. But experience is not Truth.

The ego-mind is very clever. Once you reach a level of mastery in any spiritual practice, it will convince you that you've arrived somewhere and accomplished something. Truly enlightened teachers know that volition moves you away from, not closer to, spiritual fulfillment. But the ego believes that by *doing* we are moving forward with our lives. Surrender, which is required of any earnest practitioner, is not in the vocabulary of the ego. It needs strife and effort, and it measures its spiritual progress against everyone else by constant comparison.

Of course, comparison is not limited to the area of spiritual growth. Even inside the heads of the real *nice* people (you know who you are) is a violent, hostile voice that goes unnoticed. It tears and rends, judges and depreciates. It loves to hear itself talk. It relishes criticizing others. It values its opinions, positions, prognostications, and the stories it tells. No one is exempt from the ego-mind. Yet almost no one notices it. It has become a nice suit of clothes we put on in childhood and never take off. It feels comfortable. After all, we completely *identify* with it.

The presence of ego doesn't have to be pompous and obnoxious to stifle the flow of life. Those quiet passive people who harbor their resentments and act out their rage in quiet, even pleasant ways, do it also. Consider the stereotypical couple. He's a drunk and a womanizer who is angry and out of control. She loves Jesus and goes to Bible studies and volunteers at church. Don't be deceived by the thin veneer of respectability she presents. She's up to her eyeballs in the interlocking of ego defenses with her husband. Because she's convinced she's right and he's wrong, she is probably lost. The ego-mind has white-washed her brain with a not even subtle form of arrogance.

I use a broad brush here to sound the alarm. The ego-mind must learn from its human owner that we are wise to its games and that we can see through to its underlying motives. We must reclaim our lives from this darkness once and for all. The ego is dancing with a straw hat and a cane. It loves its act. We love our act and hope you love our act, too.

I realize I'm painting a gloomy picture of the human condition. That's because it is gloomy. I'm a marriage counselor. The ego-mind is in full regalia in my office with its partner sitting there. It blames, accuses, and refuses to accept responsibility. It develops subtle, not subtle, slick, and abusive ways to attack the other. It is a place of overwhelming darkness. But never mind that. The ego cannot be shamed or embarrassed.

THE MOSAIC "ME"

It's a mind of voices, sub-personalities, arrogance, critical parents, and conditioned responses. It's a mosaic. Put all the little pieces in their proper places, and you get this familiar feeling of "me." The common connection is through the limbic system, with its emotional memory that drives perception and most goal-directed intentional behavior—and does it outside of our awareness. It was originally intended to help us survive in the wild. To do its job, it must see us as still in a wilderness of some kind, otherwise it would see nothing for which to strive.

Through associations, it invokes a repetitive litany of mental players and resources to help us guide our lives without our ever really being aware.

Above all, there is one message, one recurring theme that underlies every function it performs: "Houston, we have a problem."

The ego-mind, the mosaic mind, sees problems. Everything is a problem. Nothing is right. Fulfillment must wait until problems are solved. For the "identified thinker," life is a constant challenge to right every wrong, to fix what's broken, and to complain constantly that things are not the way the mosaic mind thinks it should be.

Watching is the way out of this primitive system. "Mere" awareness is the answer. Developing this skill takes commitment and practice, but the results are immediate and extremely gratifying. Once the identified thinker dies, new life is brought forth. It is our birthright. The world of evil we see all around us serves no other purpose than to invite us to look within. There we find the answer to all. The glue that holds all those disturbing pictures on the wall of our perception is in our heads, hiding from view. Once the light of our awareness illuminates those dark corners of conditioned thought, freedom is at hand.

After Adam and Eve were evicted from paradise for the sin of judging good and evil, angels were dispatched to guard the Tree of Life. A study of the original Hebrew reveals that the flaming swords they carried were swords that shined in all directions (Genesis 3:24). Now, why would the path to that tree be so marked? Once we are free of the arrogant judging of the limbic system and its system of ego survival, do we find there is a beacon of truth?

Awareness itself, could that be the light that shines from those swords?

Chapter 11: Witness Consciousness

*Throw out all your talking, concepts, and words! After all,
what is the mind? It is just noise that goes on inside.*

Nisargadatta Maharaj

Brian has been working on witnessing his thoughts for some time and is
sitting in front of me, telling me something has shifted for him. I can tell just
by looking at him. He seems lighter and much less agitated. He looks like a
different person in the same body.

"All I can say is wow! I feel great. I've never felt like this before in my
life. Wow!"

"Brian, congratulations, and welcome to your new life. It's nothing short
of a rebirth."

"Man, that's what it feels like. I know one thing I've never known
before."

I raise my eyebrows in interest and ask, "What's that?"

"As long as I watch, drama can't get me. I'm untouchable. Sure, there
are painful things that happen and I still feel them. Not everything makes me
ecstatic. But I don't struggle with anything anymore. And as long as I don't
take on my thoughts, I'm free."

"It's wonderful."

"You know what is interesting about it? I seem to know things. For
instance, I not only know all of the time what's truly motivating me, but I can

also see what's underlying what everyone else is doing. It's not as if I'm some kind of genius. I can just see more. That's all."

"Entering into witness consciousness is a real eye-opener. That's common to the experience."

Brian's facial expression suddenly becomes more sober. "At first it was sad. One of the first things I could see was everyone's pain. It's so obvious, the pain they're experiencing. They can't see it, but I can see that it drives everything they do. It was overwhelming at first."

"Yes, when you start witnessing your thoughts, there's no game-playing with pain anymore and it suddenly becomes very obvious what's going on around you."

"And that thing you told me to look for—the 'perceptual awakening,' you called it. Well, I can sense that, too. It's a real breakthrough. It's as if I've been looking through just one small pane of a window. Now I can see through all the panes."

"The limbic system narrows our focus to only a restricted view of the world. Now you have the opportunity to look at life with innocent perceptions – no preconceptions."

Brian sits back and gets a thoughtful look on his face. "So what's happened to my brain? Did this witness consciousness affect my brain?"

"Absolutely. Let me show you." I jump to my white board and start drawing my head with the brain inside. It looks like this:

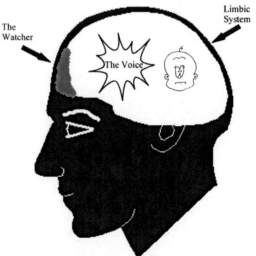

Figure 11-1 The identified thinker

"Okay, here's the brain with the limbic system —that hurt, angry, fearful five-year-old that lives in our heads. Now, the limbic system is pretty well wired up by the time we're five. There is some additional growth that happens later, but the emotional core of our first goal-directed strategies is set up by that time."

Brian nods. He has heard this much many times before.

"The problem is that since the prefrontal lobes—let's call them the 'watcher'—in a sense came along after the limbic system, this resulted in an error of identification. The limbic system was all along the driving force behind the automatic, uncontrollable thinking and the voice that yammers away in our heads all of the time. But the watcher made the mistake of thinking that the voice was its voice. So people started assuming that 'Thoughts-R-Us.' This happened due to the developmental differences between the prefrontal lobes and the limbic system. It created the 'identified thinker.'"

I continue. "Now, since you've been watching your thoughts, let's modify this drawing a little." I doodle on the board and come up with this revision.

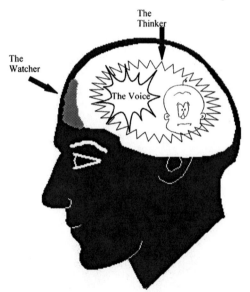

Figure 11-2 The Watcher watches the Thinker

"Since the watcher can watch thoughts, the natural conclusion would be, 'Hey, I'm not my thoughts.' You can't be anything you can watch. After watching for a little while longer, the inescapable conclusion is, 'Hey, I'm not only not my thoughts; I'm not the thinker of the thoughts, either. Thinking is happening without my intention, so I can't be the thinker.' So we can divide things up a little bit into the 'thinker' and the 'watcher.'"

I sit down for a moment and point to the board. Then I look at Brian. "How am I doing so far?"

"It makes so much sense it's scary. But I've got a simple question."

"Go ahead."

"Why do the thoughts stop when you watch them?"

"What a great question. It turns out that watching and thinking are two mutually exclusive things. The prefrontal lobes cannot do two things at once. So when you *pay attention* to anything you cannot think. When you think, you cannot pay attention."

Brian looks puzzled. "If you can't do both at once, how can you actually watch a thought?"

"Literally, you can't. You are actually watching the thought as it was the instant before. We can really only watch past thoughts. But the transition happens so fast that is seems that we are watching the actual thought formation. We literally stop the mind; switch off the *thinker*, when we switch to watching."

"So when we are thinking, we are not really in the present. Shocking!"

I have to agree with him. "Imagine the implications for humanity."

Now I add a line between the thinker and the watcher, and my drawing is finished.

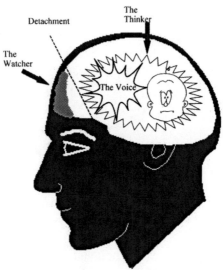

Figure 11-3 Witness Consciousness is Born

"When the inescapable reality is discovered through watching, a detachment happens and witness consciousness is born or more likely uncovered. This detachment is nothing short of a rebirth. Sometimes this happens suddenly, but usually it happens over a few weeks of concentrated thought-watching. This dis-identification or detachment from the source of thought has produced witness consciousness in you. Now you can see through the ego-mind. Its tricks, games, and deceptions are now out in the light of your own awareness."

"Okay, so here's a question for you that's been on my mind. Isn't all this Buddhism or meditation or something like that?"

I take a long breath and exhale slowly. This is a question I puzzled over for some time. Articulating my conclusions may be a little difficult for Brian, but I want to answer the question, if for no other reason than to see what answer emerges. I know that must seem funny. But I find that the "voice" wants to be an understudy that tries to feed me lines from off-stage, with me merely repeating what is said in my head. When I stopped allowing that to happen, I soon became quite surprised at the things I said. The profundity of what naturally emerged was often amazing. There seemed to be an intelligence communicating that was not my own. In that spirit, I look at Brian and begin.

"Brian, I'm not an expert on Buddhism, but let me tell you what I've observed in many meditators I've met over the years. There seems to be a belief that awareness is something that is found in the spaces between thoughts. In other words, the more quiet the mind, the more we are able to enter into that state of pure awareness. So a lot of emphasis gets put on not thinking, letting go of thought, and concentrating on the gaps between thought. So awareness, that cosmic truth, is seen as that which lies beneath all—if we can plunge far enough into the mind. But, Brian, let me ask you a question."

"Go ahead." Brian sits back as if I'm going to throw a ball at him.

"Test the truth of this statement inside, right now. Awareness can know thought, but thought can never know awareness."

Brain smiles. "Intuitively I know that's true. As the watcher, I see thoughts. The activity of the mind has to be contained within that awareness. So it seems obvious that the container would know its contents, but the contents could never know the container."

I'm amazed to hear him articulate this. I've noticed that most clients who move into witness consciousness suddenly sound more intelligent. The way Brian has summed up the situation is almost astonishing in its clarity.

"Yes, Brian, that's the heart of the matter. So in effect, what so many meditators are doing is searching for the container within the contents. This goes for the spaces between thoughts, too. It's all mind stuff. The mind is at least part of the contents of awareness. So as one meditates, the question should be who or what is watching. In meditation, I see a thought. Then I see a space between thoughts. But what just noticed that?"

Brian pipes up, "The watcher!"

"Essentially, yes; but let me just say that I prefer the term 'watching' as a synonym for 'awareness.' Nevertheless, let's get back to our friend who is meditating. He or she is using the mind to find the presence of awareness. Right?"

"That seems straightforward enough."

"So, Brian, use your knowledge of mind stuff and answer this tough question. What is motivating the meditation?" I sit back and notice a smug thought pass from the ego-mind. It was something to the effect that I'm betting he'll have to struggle with this for some time. With that thought comes a hook to feel smug. I notice this, and as I do the mental fodder evaporates.

Brian sits for a moment and then looks at me. "I'm tempted to say 'ego.' Intuitively I know that's the answer, but I'm not sure I can explain why."

"By Jove, you've done it! I wasn't sure you could get that. Of course, the answer has to be ego, which is the limbic system. That's where nearly all emotionally oriented, goal-directed behavior is generated. So what's happening with meditation or any spiritual practice is that it becomes an effort of the ego-mind to get somewhere or accomplish something. So the entire enterprise gets hijacked by the primitive brain. It literally becomes ego trying to discover the source of pure awareness *within itself*. Put another way, it becomes our effort to become God's god."

Brian gasps and says, "You're right. Oh, my God. Those poor people, they're being led astray by their ego-mind."

"It's even worse than that. Their ego becomes "spiritualized" in the process. Since for the meditator the mind must be the container of truth, as they become better meditators they must by extension have more truth in that container. The ego begins to see itself as the source of truth and the person is lost. Spiritual pride keeps them from ever questioning their achievement, and surrender never happens. This is way an awakened teacher is so important. They can help the persona avoid this mistake."

"From the standpoint of witness consciousness, this all makes perfect sense. Obviously, some meditators never shift into what you call watching." Brian has a look of concern on his face.

"I can tell it worries you, and it should. It's even worse than that, I'm afraid. Imagine a meditator sitting in the lotus position watching their thoughts and the gaps between thoughts. All of a sudden the 'voice' says, 'Hey, I'm doing a really good job watching my thoughts.' Since the person has never distinguished that voice as a thought, they believe it's them talking to themselves. Instead, as we know, it's the ego-mind talking. Even meditation has been hijacked by thought in a way that's so slick the person never notices it."

"They think they're witnessing in meditation and they're still the identified thinker."

"The proof is that once the meditation is over, they go home and get into an argument with their spouse, right back into thought-identification. If we can't see mind patterns in real life, seeing thoughts in meditation does little good."

"Okay, but I have a question, then. If this awareness that meditators are searching for in the spaces between thoughts isn't the foundation upon which thoughts appear, what is it? Or better yet where is it?"

"Pure awareness is the container, not the substrata. Therefore, it is much more intimate to us than we've ever imagined. It's attached to our nose and is as plain as the nose on our faces. It's a lot like looking for the toy in the cereal box. The box is the entire container. You paw through it looking for the toy, moving the cereal aside as you go deeper and deeper only to find the bottom eventually. If you were looking for the box by looking for the bottom, wouldn't it have been much simpler to realize that the bottom is part of the container which is all around the cereal? We don't have to paw our way through the cereal of the mind creating a hole into which we thrust our seeing. The 'seeing' is the container. If we want to experience awareness, it's right here right now. We needn't contort our body and nearly put ourselves to sleep to discover it."

#

Pat and Angie sit down. Pat says, "I can see now. I understand what you've been saying. I now know what being the *witness* means. I do feel separate from thought whenever I remember to watch."

"Me too," says Angie.

"Well, congratulations and welcome to a new world."

Pat says, "Yeah, but there's a catch."

"What's that?" I ask.

"You have to remember."

"Yes," says Angie. "If you don't remember to watch, you go right back into it. Before you know it, your head has turned on and you're into the daydream again."

"That's very important. We must remember to be vigilant, to be watchful. You know, the New Testament is full of references to being watchful. I believe what you're referring to is exactly what the scriptures are referring to. When you are being the witness you are awake, watchful. Paul even says don't sleep as others do. So when we forget to watch, we go back to sleep."

Pat looks reflective and speaks up, "I notice that when I forget and go to sleep, I go right back into the drama. But then I *remember* and I can see instantly what I've been doing."

"I have that experience, too." says Angie, "But I notice that the time-frame is getting shorter. I'm able to catch myself quicker and quicker. And actually, I've noticed one other thing."

"What's that, Angie?" I love listening to them. Being the witness is such a full experience, and it arouses a lot of curiosity when it's really taking root in a person. The more they become sensitive to and analyze their experience, the more I know that this new consciousness is taking hold.

"I notice that I feel a shift when I watch, and another when I forget and allow myself to become lost in thought."

Pat looks at her a little funny. "I feel a shift, too. I either remember to do it or I don't. It feels different."

"No, I don't mean that. I know what you mean and I notice that, too. What I'm talking about is a feeling of literally going away. When I go into my head I feel like I'm no longer present in any way. I know that my mind and body are still holding all of the senses steady as if I'm still in the world, so to speak. But it's really a feeling of having left the building and the scene is still being held in front of me—almost as a fantasy of the senses in a way. Meanwhile, I'm gone into my head." She looks at me inquiringly. "Do you know what I mean?"

I smile. "It's hard to explain isn't it? I know exactly what you mean. When you're identifying with thought, you're gone. You're asleep. You've entered into the world of drama. The moment you identify, you go away. At first it feels subtle. After a while, it's jarring and unpleasant."

Pat looks at me and asks, "Doesn't it get easier to remember?"

"With practice, of course. But there is a danger, and I want to go over it carefully with you."

"Okay," they say in unison and sit back..

I wipe my brow with both hands. "Now, you've both moved from being the full-time identified thinker, to the self-observer, and now to witness consciousness. With this comes a 'knowing' or a new awareness of life. You're able to look with innocent perception. You can see through your mind. You can see your true motives. You can see others and what motivates them—their unconsciousness, and their pain.

"But there's a danger. It comes with the thought that you *know* something. As soon as we start thinking that we *know*, that's when the ego comes in and assures us that we've got it and we don't really need to work at it anymore.

"We don't lose the *knowing,* but the ego usurps the entire process and gradually we go back into the madness, into the drama. We may even use our new perspective as a weapon against others. The world is full of people who have had legitimate awakening experiences and are now being used by the limbic system as a tool to survive at everyone else's expense."

Angie has a bit of a look of horror on her face. "How do we prevent that?"

"There are a couple things you can do. First, it requires a lot of individual intention to stay awake. We need to constantly remind ourselves to watch and not identify with thought. We must continue to experience ourselves as awareness and not as the thinker. We must continue to expand our attitude of surrender and acceptance and not allow the ego-mind to promise future fulfillment. This takes vigilance and commitment to the awakening you have experienced.

"But beyond that, you have another avenue to keep awake and deepen your experience." I pause expectantly.

Pat and Angie look at one another and back to me questioningly.

"You have one another. Every possible thing that could seduce you back into unconsciousness comes up in the relationship. You can help one another stay awake. When one person goes to sleep, the other can stay awake and practice not getting sucked into the other person's unconscious patterns. Every encounter is an opportunity to practice witness consciousness, and to go deeper into those things that prevent us from our true inheritance."

Pat asks, "Are you talking about the Lion and Unicorn patterns?"

"The Lion and Unicorn model is just a road map. Its purpose is nothing more than to point in the direction of what the mind is probably doing. Being the *witness* takes you outside of the problem-system. Problems are only related to thought, and the witness is beyond and before thought."

"You know, I'm a bit confused about witnessing and how it relates to self-observation and thought," Angie says. "I need to get the relationships laid out so I understand one from another. I mean in my experience, I understand the difference. But I'm not sure I get the big picture. Can you help me clear this up? You know what I mean?"

I get up out of my chair and pick up a marker. "Angie, let me try to lay this out and see if it clarifies things a bit."

I stand at my white board and draw a table. I start from the bottom and it looks like this:

Label	Experience	State of Awareness
Witness Consciousness	Watching	Detached from the Thinker
The "Observer of Self"	I am observing myself	Conditioned Patterns
The "Identified Thinker"	I am my thoughts	The content of thought

Table 11-1: Levels of Consciousness

"Okay, when you first came in to see me you were at this bottom level, the *Identified Thinker*. Since you identified yourself with each thought that arose in your mind, your state of awareness was restricted to the content of your thought. And even today on a moment-by-moment basis, the temptation to slip back into thought-identification is a strong pull that still can capture us if we're not vigilant.

"Now," I point to the second row from the bottom, "when you came in and I showed you your unconscious thought patterns . . ."

Angie interjects, "You mean the Lion and the Unicorn."

"Yes, you began to have a powerful experience of Self-Observation. This meant that you learned to see the patterns of perceptions, feelings, and defensive behaviors that came from your conditioning. You even started to see how that conditioning came from your early years when the limbic system was first getting dramatically wired up. The ability to self-observe is clearly a step up in consciousness or awareness. Most people never really see their patterns."

"Are the prefrontal lobes doing that?" asks Pat.

"Right," I reply. "In a real way, self-observation brings the prefrontal lobes out of dormancy. We begin to exercise self-referencing in a new and more powerful way."

"But that's nothing compared to watching your thoughts," says Angie.

"Right, each level up the ladder brings with it an entirely new perspective on life." I point to the next row up. "After a period of 'watching,' we pop into Witness Consciousness. Now our experience is that of watching and we experience ourselves as being detached from the Thinker. In a very powerful sense, then, we disidentify with the limbic system. The conditioned mind has no authority over us."

I turn to Pat and Angie and conclude, "And that is where you are today. Your perception is no longer a captive of the voice in your head. And you are able to *live* life without *thinking* life all the time. Not buying into thought brings with it a peace and calmness and an effortlessness. Life begins to just flow along without our resistance damming up the river."

"Thanks," says Angie, "That does put it in perspective. But I have a question."

"Shoot."

"It looks like there's something missing."

"Something missing?" I ask.

"Yes. You see above the level of witness consciousness there's a row with nothing in it. Does that mean there's another level?"

"Oops! I let the cat out of the bag. Yes, there is another level; but we're out of time and we'll have to talk about that another day."

Angie leaps to her feet. "You can't do this to me! Please tell me. I'll go nuts! Damn you *shrinks*, you think you know it all." Angie is trying hard to suppress her giggle while giving me a hard time.

So in the spirit of the ribbing, I chime in, "Angie, we do know it all. After all, I have a Ph.D. That means I'm *much* smarter than you."

"Oh, my God! Pat, let's get out of here. I know he got his degree from a matchbook cover. Let's find someone who really knows what he's doing. These people only get into psychology because they're screwed up to begin with."

Pat turns to me and winks while he rolls his eyes. Angie grabs him and pulls him out the door.

Chapter 12: Witness Thought Therapy™

*In our rush to find a better situation in time, we trample over
the flower of beingness that presents itself in every moment.*

Tony Parsons

To say that traditional psychotherapy doesn't work is a bit of an overstatement, but it's true. Often people spend months if not years to no avail. Couples counseling has an even more dismal record of success. That's not to say that there's something wrong with therapists who are trying to help. All the studies that have looked at therapy and its effects agree that the most powerful force for change is the relationship between the client and the therapist. That would suggest that the mental health and emotional maturity of the therapist are critical in whether or not the client gets anything out of the relationship.

From a theoretical perspective, most traditional methods have a lot to do with "working through" emotions associated with family dynamics that are left over from the early impressionable days of childhood development. There are cognitive techniques that are more oriented toward thoughts, thinking, and the beliefs associated with thinking. Then there are therapeutic interventions that resolve to stop thoughts and challenge thoughts. What is the result of all of this? In some rare cases, full or partial success can be achieved.

The brain is a nonlinear, dynamic, chaotic system full of strange attractors. Don't let the term chaos confuse you. It's a misconception to think of chaos in this sense as disorder. In fact, this chaos is the very essence of order. The patterns that emerge in the firing of billions of neurons dictate that our experience of life is self repeating. We have the same experiences in different circumstances over and over. Therapy, from this perspective, hopes to reshape and reorganize territory within an attractor landscape laid down in early childhood and possibly even from genetics, thereby forming new attractor patterns. In human terms, this means new perspectives, perception, and ultimately behaviors.

Another way of thinking about the recursive quality of brain dynamics is to revisit ideas about perception that I presented earlier in this book. The preafferent or anticipatory quality of perception boils down to this: If the only tool you have is a hammer, everything looks like a nail. In other words, the recursive quality of "problems" in our lives, as we have always known intuitively, is a self-fulfilling prophecy.

Our beliefs are the motivators behind actions that are intended to produce results that confirm those beliefs. Therapy should be designed to get us out of that loop. The unintended result of much of therapy is to keep us stuck in the loop, however. It does this by having us relive the emotional pain that is the genesis of the beliefs to begin with. Then, in the act of actually triggering the recursive pattern, we are asked to behave differently.

Once in a while, this actually has the unexpected consequence of providing just enough impetuousness to actually shift the entire problem system out of its equilibrium. Unfortunately this happens in a vast minority of cases. As a therapist, you never know exactly what you'll say or how you'll say it that might provide the sea change for the person in front of you. More often than not, unwitting therapists succumb by being sympathetic to the problem-system and relegating themselves to the role of an advice-giver.

Most therapy tries to work with the client's resistance to change. In effect, what we're trying to do is to move a boulder in the road with dynamite instead of simply routing around the obstacle. Trying to impose new order on a chaotic system has been proven to be nearly impossible. New order in a nonlinear, dynamic system *emerges*; it can't be *imposed*.

Witness Thought Therapy™ happily resolves this problem by removing the person completely from the problem-system. This is based on the axiom that no problem can be solved from within the drama of the problem.

Take the following example. Let's say you were raised in an alcoholic family. It is well known that the expression of anger is verboten in these circumstances. You learn to express your rage by become passive and procrastinating. Procrastination becomes an expression of anger, and it doesn't even look like anger, does it? But it can really screw up somebody else's life. What is really slick about it is that the passive aggressive procrastinator isn't consciously aware of what they are doing. They just feel the pressure of "being on time" which they naturally resist. Eventually the other person or people will be driven to frustration over the procrastination. What ensues is an explosive fit of anger. The procrastinator has the satisfaction of controlling others emotionally, punishing them, and vicariously seeing anger vented.

That is a very powerful subconscious agenda, and by the time you're forty years old, it is certain the pattern is still active. We would assume, in our ignorance, that simply learning time-management would cure the problem. But every time anything in our environment looks like those things that triggered the original motivation to procrastinate, we are helpless. Good intentions cannot overcome the attractor basin created by early experiences in an alcoholic family.

As I write this, I have someone in my practice who makes a to-do list every day and then resists doing everything on the list. Why? Because at a powerful level of mind that process fits the pattern of being told what to do. All the person's passive resistance comes up to divert efforts toward more self-rewarding endeavors. The voice in the head is saying, "No one tells me what to do." So much for the to-do list and other self-help techniques, books, and workshops.

So in summary, what a lot of traditional therapy does is to lead the person into the drama of the problem system. This may be procrastination, anger, depression, or whatever the motivation for therapy in the first place. Then, from within the drama, they are lead to try to see things differently. This might actually work once in a while. But this is certainly not something that can be predicted. What is more likely is that the person will go into the drama and then, from within that system, see that the problem is really related to a learned pattern left over from some childhood programming. In that moment of *seeing*, the dots are connected and the person has an "ah ha" experience that lifts them out of the recursive nature of the problem. Since the problem no longer relates to the original frame of reference (their current life circumstances), the problem in that context no longer exists.

From this perspective, let's go back to the procrastinator. If the procrastination is seen as a survival technique left over from the alcoholic family, the person reframes the entire problem. Looking over a to-do list suddenly becomes an experience of resisting my controlling mother. The spell is broken and the problem is no longer a problem.

But what really happens in these moments of epiphany? My experience with this process is that an epiphany is a *seeing*. And this is what really happens when the person lifts themselves out of the problem system. A *seeing* takes place. Before this, there's no *seeing*. There's simply the unconscious repetition of (c) a learned behavior that's preceded by (a) the voice in the head that dictates a meaning to us, which is followed by (b) a painful feeling that we don't want to feel. This results in a behavior whose genesis lies hidden, due to the mental dullness that has been created by thousands and thousands of repetitions of the pattern.

One of my clients one day referred to this sort of a pattern when he suddenly said, "No wonder I couldn't see it. It was too obvious!"

The "Voice" Speaks ➤ Perception ➤ Feelings ➤ Defensive Behavior

Figure 12-1 Unconscious cognitive process.

Figure 12-1 shows the process. As with the procrastinator, the voice speaks, saying, "Mom is trying to control me." Perception then becomes the substance of the voice, I am being controlled. This feels like pressure. The defense against pressure is to resist. Procrastination is passive resistance.

The very definition of "unconscious mind" is that this process, which is established in early childhood (before five years of age), is repeated over and over again, year after year. It's not exactly unconscious. It's *super*conscious. It's so all-encompassing and familiar that we eventually delete it from our awareness. I venture that this happens to nearly everything that we deem as unconscious. It is so automatic that the pilot no longer has an incentive to pay attention to it. We have an additional incentive to ignore this process. It's always associated with emotional pain. Who wants to feel pain?

What calls this into question is when our lives become so painful that the level of pain we're hiding from becomes eclipsed by the pain of keeping the hidden process itself. You finally dial the phone and come to my office, or somebody's office. The bottom line is that we don't want to know until we have an incentive to know. Then we're willing to look. This is driven by pain. We want relief, so we're willing to wake up and look at the pain we're hiding from.

PROCESS VS. CONTENT

It has always been known that one's ability to have insight is critical for the success of therapy. It is also known that insight is one of the first abilities that is sacrificed in a stressful childhood. Too much stress and the finer abilities of the prefrontal lobes are compromised, to the point where the person is doomed to be on the "Jerry Springer Show" for the rest of their lives.

For what are we to use our vaunted ability for insight? Too much therapy has been devoted toward the content of the problem. Many people who come to my office are highly insulted if I won't spend many sessions listening ad nauseam to the details of the content, the drama. When I was in graduate school, much was made of concentrating on process instead of content. I don't remember being educated well on how to dissect the process. And yet the key to freedom from problems is to *see* what we're doing to create the problem.

Process is a lot like a golfer who wants to cure his slice. We all know that the slice is being caused by a flaw in the process of swinging the golf club. That being the case, it's impossible to solve the problem by complaining about the slice or the effects of the slice on the pleasure of the game of golf. It's obviously an issue of process. The golfer must *see* what he or she is doing to create the problem. That's why so many instructors use video equipment.

The golf metaphor applies equally to psychotherapy. Clients in counseling must also *see* what they are doing. Life happens in a variety of ways that are painful, or not, to all of us. But the suffering we create from the pain is clearly a result of the process we use to think about the pain.

WITNESS THOUGHT THERAPY™ IS DIFFERENT

There are other therapeutic techniques that might be considered similar to witnessing. These are "mindfulness," cognitive behavior therapy (CBT) and "externalizing." Let's look at them one at a time.

Mindfulness or being mindful is defined as present moment awareness or paying attention. You are not reflecting, judging, or thinking. You are simply observing the moment. Mindfulness is associated with Buddhism and is used as a form of meditation. In this form of meditation the practitioner is mindful of every breath. In addition, the practice of mindfulness is promoted by such people as author and medical researcher Dr. Jon Kabat-Zinn who developed the Mindfulness-Based Stress Reduction program. Mindfulness can be extremely relaxing and helpful. It is a technique that can benefit any type of therapy.

In his book, *Full Catastrophe Living*, Kabat-Zinn says, "Just being aware of the mind that thinks is knows all the time is a major step toward learning how to see through your opinions and perceive things as they actually are."

While I whole heartedly endorse mindfulness and its benefits as an adjunct to therapy, there is a distinction I would like to make. Witnessing thought specifically focuses the attention on the "voice in the head." It is a form of mindfulness in that respect, but it is done all the time with eyes open and in the everyday walk of life. You do not need to seek repose or the isolation of meditation.

If witnessing the "voice" is practiced with determination and the watching is done as often as can be remembered not to get lost in thought, the practice produces witness consciousness in a relatively short period of time (weeks). The same cannot be said of mindfulness.

To my Buddhist oriented friends, this all seems a bit too easy. Any of them that have transitioned into witness consciousness have done so only after two or more years of meditation with an excellent teacher. They simply cannot believe that watching the voice produces results so fast. Sadly, many of them think they are in witness consciousness because they have done so much mediation. For them mindfulness slipped into the ego realm of getting somewhere or trying to accomplish something.

Let's look quickly at Cognitive Behavioral Therapy. CBT was developed by Aaron Beck and has the distinction of being the only form of therapy that has been documented in studies to produce results.

CBT uses a thought record or other journaling technique to catalog situations, moods, and the "automatic" thoughts that produce the symptoms of depression, anxiety or whatever the client's presenting problem. The automatic or "hot thought" then is analyzed in terms of evidence that supports the thought and evidence that refutes the thought.

The thought might be, "I'm not good enough," which would be tied to a core belief. The person would then go through an exercise to determine if in the real world of today's experience that belief is actually true. It always proves not to be true so the client then practices substituting an alternative or "balanced" thought like, "Even thought the situation might be challenging, I have met similar challenges before."

CBT is often very effective in solving long standing psychological problems. I have used it on clients and seen nearly miraculous results. It is like witnessing thought in that it isolates thought and builds awareness of the process of problem formation. While CBT, like mindfulness, is highly effective, it does not produce the dramatic shift in consciousness that witnessing the "voice" does. It does produce a shift into "self-observation," which starts the movement of a person out of the self-repeating patterns of the ego-mind.

Externalizing was developed by a gifted therapist out of New Zealand by the name of Michael White. It's a therapeutic technique that assumes that the person is not the problem that the problem is external. If I were externalizing someone's depression, I might say, "When depression whispers in your ear, what does it say?"

From this perspective the person sees that they are separate from the problem, that the problem is attacking or oppressing them. This is as opposed to being a person with some pathology. It is a form of dis-identification with the problem. This puts the problem in a completely different frame and empowers the person to become resourceful in overcoming their issue.

The key principle here is dis-identification. This is shared with witnessing thought. However, witnessing thought is far more powerful since problem formation begins with thought. In effect witnessing turns the process of externalization inside out. *We* become external to the entire problem system. From this perspective problems don't exist unless we are seduced into entering into the system of problem formation. What is that? We identify ourselves with disembodied thoughts that only lead to drama. The thought, "I'm not good enough," has no life of its own unless we grab hold of it.

So like CBT and mindfulness, externalizing produces a transition to a form of self-observation while witnessing thought produces an even greater transformation.

THE MAN WHO MISTOOK HIS THOUGHT FOR A HAT

It's not far from the truth of the human experience to say that there's nothing wrong with life unless we think about it. Life is *painful* at times, but *suffering* comes from the thinking we do around the pain. How we interpret what is happening to us is the source of drama and problems in our life. As shown in Figure 12-1, thinking, most of which is the voice in our heads, triggers feelings that are painful. From this springs our conclusion that we have a problem. But without thinking there's no problem. This is clear.

It sounds like I'm making a case to stop thinking. I'm not. That's actually impossible. Stopping thought is a lot like quieting a child by putting your hand over his mouth. It only makes the problem a thousand times bigger.

I am, however, making a case for not taking thought seriously. Anyone can be unhappy, but the ability to make ourselves unhappy has to be learned. What is this learning? It is the constant repetition of unhelpful thought-patterns in our heads; but more than that, it is our continued *identification* with thought. We think thoughts are commands that must be obeyed. And we do this automatically without noticing it.

I was explaining all this to a client one day who suddenly looked at me and said, "It never occurred to me that a thought is just a thought." She, like all of us, had mistaken a thought for a hat. What do you do with a hat? You put it on. What do you do with a thought? We accept it like a relative who shows up at our door without an invitation. We say to ourselves that we must let him in since he has nowhere else to go.

This basic mistake has been the downfall of humanity. But this concept is the cornerstone of a new vista of the mind and how to solve problems. Problems are not to be solved at all. Instead, the thoughts that create them are not to be taken on. This leads to a leap in the process vs. content concept.

As stated before, we're much better off if we pay attention to the process of problem-creation rather than the content. Let's forget about problems for a moment. What if instead of paying attention to the process of problem-formation we paid attention to the process of thought-identification. This is one step prior to problems. Since problems come from thought-identification, what if we study the process of thought-formation?

This requires witness consciousness. If we watch a thought, we find that the thought persists only if we identify with it. If we merely watch it, it ceases to exist. If we are expert watchers, it follows that watching stops problems. There is no thought left to cause a problem. The problem thought-pattern may still be there like a rock in the road. But rather than move the rock, we just take a helicopter instead: Thought-watching stops the entire chain that involves thoughts that lead to a chain of thoughts, which leads to drama, which emerges as a problem.

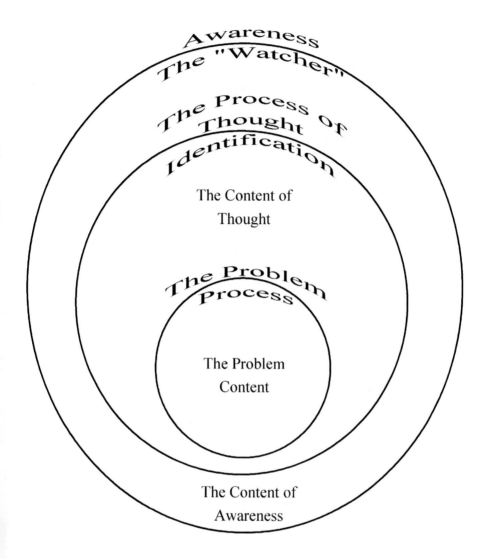

Figure 12-2 The process of problem formation

Figure 12-2 shows that in order for problems to have content, there must be a learned process that forms the content. This process of problem-formation is a function of the content of thoughts with which we identify. But the giant irony of this system is that when awareness is focused on thought without identification, no problems are possible.

Lest you think I've taken leave of my senses, let me explain something about the thoughts we're talking about. These are the random and associative thoughts that are under the direction of the ego-mind, i.e. the limbic system. In contrast to them, if I ask you to go inside your head and say your name to yourself, you are picking up a valuable tool called the *dialogical self* and you are initiating an intentional thought; if you must travel across town and you review directions in your head, again you're using thinking as a tool. Thoughts such as these last two are not the thoughts I'm talking about.

I am talking about the trash that involuntarily fills our heads. If a man came to your door selling bags of trash, you probably wouldn't buy any. Just because a thought arises in our heads doesn't mean we reach for our wallets, either. And yet, from time immemorial, we've been paying through the nose for any thought that happens to come along. We pay with the consequences of living a tortured life filled only with the content of our thoughts.

But simply watching thoughts, although it is powerful and produces an awakening, isn't always enough to extricate us from some of our deepest issues. This is where the help of an awakened therapist comes in.

WITNESS THOUGHT THERAPY™: TRICKING THE LIMBIC SYSTEM

By now it must be obvious that step one of the process of Witness Thought Therapy™ is to enter into witness consciousness by simply watching thought instead of automatically identifying with it. Understanding what this means in practice can take some time. It's not unusual for a client to spend two full sessions just getting the hang of what it means to watch a thought. Many clients do, however, get this step in a few minutes. In any case, the time doesn't matter. The important point is to *get it*.

The next step in the process is to practice thought-watching as diligently as possible. This can be very difficult for some. We forget so easily. During this period of learning, the biggest obstacle is just to remember to look. Gradually, with commitment, this gets easier and more frequent. Eventually, the detachment of witness consciousness kicks in and we're ready for the next step.

The experience of entering witness consciousness is both enlightening and liberating. Often times a person easily sees and resolves long-standing problems. But some of the most insidious still can be elusive. This is where I come in.

I will have the person present the problem to me. It always involves an emotional reaction to an external event—usually a person. These are almost always typical Lion/Unicorn patterns, since they are the most deep-seated.

I interview the person to find out the potential emotional trigger. It usually turns out to be "when he said this" or "when she did that." Then I simply repeat the pattern while the person remains in awareness and watches the ego-mind. Usually the voice speaks right away and the pattern unfolds completely while the person watches. This is usually quite a weighty and revealing therapeutic experience. The power of watching the pattern unfold from the witness vantage point releases the person from the grip of the pattern, and it will never have quite the same influence it did for so long.

Each person usually carries two or three of these patterns. Repeated rehearsals of the pattern reveal more and more psychodynamic information about the conditioning of the automatic mind. For the participant, it's a lot like seeing the answer to a mystery revealed.

Why is this so easy? Two factors are in play. First, the ego-mind can be easily tricked into revealing the pattern. The limbic system operates by means of association. All the therapist needs to do is play the role of the trigger. Second, witness consciousness takes the person completely outside the problem-system and gives them a front-row seat to watch the process unfold. But also, in a very real sense, in becoming the witness the person also becomes their own therapist. The insight, the meaning, and the integration of the information is done automatically through awareness.

I have a bit of an advantage over the participant in that I've been through this exercise a few times. I know the tricks of the mind, and I can help the person negotiate the terrain traveled by so many I've seen before. But the power of witnessing is the real healer.

Once this takes place, the person is done with therapy except for one thing. Witnessing is a doorway to something much greater. It must be nurtured and cultivated, or the person will inadvertently step back into the madness of identified thought. It can take months, even years, for this new sight to be integrated into one's moment-by-moment experience. Watching the content of ego-mind and object-consciousness in the end raises one question: If I'm not my thoughts, who am I?

Chapter 13: Witness Thought Therapy™ Unplugged

In our enlightened ignorance we being to see the heavy toll
that ignorance exacts from us and from those around us.

James Finely

I am looking at fifteen-year-old Brian, wondering how he took what I told him last week. His mom brought him into therapy months ago because he was having trouble in school and their relationship had pretty badly deteriorated. Their fighting had escalated and he had become more and more abusive. Plus, he absolutely refused to do homework.

Through many sessions together, we've developed a good rapport. His relationship with his mother has improved but his homework, although a bit more on track, is still a source of concern.

What surprised me when I became a therapist was how well I was able to relate to and get along with teenagers. I would have bet good money that there was no way I could ever be effective with adolescents or teens. I was pleasantly surprised to find that I took to it easily and the kids seemed to enjoy my style.

Last week I told Brian the story of my awakening experience and the incredible "dark night of the soul" which had preceded it. When I got to the part of my story where I describe the new world into which I had seemingly awakened, he appeared to become transfixed. I remember the look in his eyes when I described having no more fear of death. I had never seen him so serious.

Most teenagers are pretty involved in their lives. Cell phones, video games, girlfriends, boyfriends, and the constant struggle with parents leave little time or incentive for self-reflection. I had tried to introduce Brian to watching his thoughts, but I could tell he was much more interested in other things. Or so I thought.

"So, Brian, I'm interested to see if my little story had any impact on you."

"I'm watching my thoughts."

This is significant. He took my narrative so seriously he went immediately to watching his thoughts.

"I'm impressed."

"I feel calmer."

"So what happens to the thoughts when you watch them?"

"Just like the first exercises we did. They disappear."

I smile and reflect on the process that I teach clients. The discovery that awareness of mind makes the mind stop still amazes me. But even when a client practices this until they enter into the detachment that I call "witness consciousness," there are deeper underlying patterns that must be dealt with. These patterns are Lion/Unicorn patterns. The patterns are simple, but they are so pervasive that they're often hidden for even the most aware client. That's where I come in.

Looking at Brian, I'm wondering if it might be time to try step two in Witness Thought Therapy™. "So, shall we try this witnessing out to see if we can find out what's underneath some of the challenges you're facing?"

Brian grins and says, "That sounds like fun."

"Okay, so here's what I want you to do. Just relax and don't try to analyze anything. I'm going to say something that will trigger a pattern in your limbic system, and you be the watcher. In other words, watch whatever happens and let it happen spontaneously."

I know that telling someone to "be spontaneous" is a paramount example of a paradoxical instruction. But I'm hoping he'll get the idea.

"Okay, I'm ready. What are we going to work on?"

"How about homework?"

"Whoa, that is a problem. I'm interested to see what comes to my mind."

"Good, okay, here goes. You just watch now."

I muster a little authority in my voice and I command him, "Brian, it's time to do your homework!"

"I don't want to. That's the first thing that came to mind."

"Right, but we're missing a step. You're zeroing in on the resistance right?"

"Right. I'm not going to do it!"

"Okay, but think about our cognitive process that we had on the board the other day. Remember that perception leads to feelings which lead to defensive behavior? That resistance of 'I don't want to' is the defense. Do you see?"

"I think so, but I'm not sure."

"Well, in order for you to resist what I said, you have to make meaning out of it first, right?"

Brain nods. "I have to make some distinction out of what you said. I have to interpret it. Is that what you mean?"

"Right, perception – perception is meaning and the voice gives us perception. But it goes by in our minds so fast that we don't notice it. So we have to slow the process down a little. Now let's do it again and just let the voice, that dialogical self, speak."

"Okay."

"Brian, it's time to do your homework."

Brain appears deep in thought. "I'm not getting anything. Try saying it another way."

"Okay, you need to do your homework!"

Suddenly his eyes light up and he declares, "I'm being controlled."

"The voice has spoken!" So often this happens. The voice just takes over as if the person has been hypnotized or somehow set aside. That injunction from the limbic system just speaks the words of meaning.

When I first tried this step in Witness Thought Therapy™, I would encourage the person to be the watcher, to witness the activity of the mind. My expectation was that they would hear the internal voice say the key words of perception "like I will be rejected." To my surprise that's not what happened. What more often happened was that the voice would actually vocalize the injunction "I'm going to be rejected" "I'm being pressured" or words to that effect. This would then start the process of the pattern that ends in some kind of a defensive stance. Usually the person is just as surprised as I am by what jumps out of their mouth.

"Okay, now go deep inside. Who's trying to control you?"

"My mom," he says as if he's just discovered the answer to a mystery.

"Okay, Brian, so let's look at what we've discovered. When you were young, it appeared that your mother was trying to control you. You learned to defend that by resisting and not doing anything she wanted you to do, or something to that effect. So since the limbic system formed an attractor pattern back then around the perception of being controlled, now anything that even remotely looks like that is swept into that attractor. The voice in your head speaks, telling you the meaning of your experience, and you resist."

"Radical! You mean I think my mother is trying to control me all the time?"

"Yes. I know it sounds crazy, but your limbic system thinks the entire world is your mother."

"No!"

"This trance that we go into is so big and pervasive that it controls us all the time. It feels so comfortable that we don't notice it or question it. The point is that awareness of the pattern is your only chance to have your life back. Watching your thoughts takes you into a level of consciousness where that voice telling you something is controlling you is amusing rather than trance-producing."

"Okay, I get it. I guess I'd better practice watching my thoughts more. This is stupid. I've got my teacher confused with my mother."

"It's worse than that. Since this is a Unicorn pattern, that feeling like you're being pressured or controlled, you'll marry someone who fits the pattern. Your conditioned mind will constantly be responding as if your wife is your mother. Awareness is the only way out of the prison."

#

Angie has asked for a private session without Pat in attendance. She walks into the room and sits down.

"I'm so glad you would see me. I didn't know what else to do."

Even though I don't want to engage in speculation, I can sense my ego-mind trying to paint scenarios in my head—an affair, a financial reversal, a tragedy of some kind. If I bought in to any of these lines of thinking I would be in the imagined future instead of being present with Angie.

"Ok, tell me what's up."

"Well, it was about 2:30 in the morning the other night. I suddenly woke up and Pat wasn't in the bed with me. I got up and could see light coming from the study. I guess I can make this short. I caught him downloading porn on the Internet. I was devastated. I started to scream at him. We had a horrible fight."

"Okay, and how can I help?"

She looks at me like I'm crazy and says, "You can help me find the right words to tell him he's wrong to do that. I've always been militant about porn. I think it's wrong. I think it's immoral."

I'm sorely tempted to leave presence and react to this. How can I get her to see what she's doing? All I can do is to stay present and watch my thoughts; and if there's anything that might help, it will emerge into the space between us.

"Angie, you said that you started screaming at him. At 2:30 in the morning, that must have scared hell out of him."

"I don't care. He hurt me and he's wrong for doing what he did. Everyone knows that women only get violent because a man did first."

I notice that she is recruiting "everyone" to be on her side, and then using his behavior as an excuse to justify her attack on him. "So he attacked you first? Tell me how he managed to do that?"

Again she stares at me like I'm not getting it at all. "The porn, the porn was the attack. He knows I don't like it."

"Angie, you and I have known each other for a long time. We've done some awfully good work together. Wouldn't you agree?"

Angie nods, if only reluctantly, with a sullen look on her face. "I know what you're going to say."

"What am I going to say?"

"You're going to say that I need to look at my reaction to all of this. That I'm wrong."

"Oh, please. Give me a break. Stop feeling sorry for yourself. Do you want to be right or be free?"

"Free, I want to be free." She buries her head in her hands and sobs. I hand her the ever-ready box of tissues. "But Pat is wrong. What he's doing is wrong."

"And your job is to be in his life to show him how wrong he is? Like that works. All you're doing is justifying your judgment against him. So let me ask you a question. Is it possible that your attacking him at 2:30 in the morning is morally equivalent to what he did to you? Which was more the act of violence?"

"Yes, but he isn't supposed to do that. We've talked about it and he agreed."

It's extremely difficult to reason with someone who is in a defensive reaction, especially someone who thinks they're right. Normally I recommend that people wait until their partner is calm and has their wits about them before they try to talk to them. When someone is defensive, they are usually unreachable. Unfortunately, I don't have that luxury. I must try to pull her back from the insanity of thought-identification, back into Presence.

"Angie, think. You're a Lion. Pat's a Unicorn. Why would he agree with you?"

Angie stops for a moment and appears to be lost in thought. I detect a tiny shaking of her head as if she's trying to shake off the effects of her defensive fugue.

"Oh shit!" she exclaims.

"What?" I ask, as if I don't already know what she just saw.

"He was just agreeing to that to appease me, wasn't he?"

I nod my head. "That would be my guess. It was a setup all along."

"Oh, my God! He didn't want the conflict. That would mean I'm experiencing shame, wouldn't it?"

"So would you like to process through this, or are you not done with your reaction?"

Angie looks at me and nods. "I want to process it. My God, what's wrong with me?"

"Nothing is wrong. Everything is right. Our reactions serve only one purpose, and that is to point us deeper inside ourselves. It tells us nothing about the other person. Reactions are an invitation to go deeper."

"What is it about porn? Why does it hurt so much?" Angie asks in exasperation.

"Are you ready to look and see?" I wonder if she really is. Staking out a position against something perceived to be morally wrong is so self-righteous. It's hard to pull away from the ego's pride.

Angie pulls herself together. A look of determination is now in her eyes. "Okay. Let's go."

"Alright, you move into witness consciousness and notice what your mind does. Anything is significant. Also, you might just spontaneously say something that will be significant. So here we go."

I make a motion with my right hand. "Pat is looking at porn. Now notice what your mind does, or listen for what the dialogical self says."

Angie focuses inside, and it looks like she's struggling to come up with something.

"Angie, let it go. Don't struggle. You are merely the *watcher*. So there's no work for you to do here. The automatic mind will do it for you through association."

"I'm trying too hard, aren't I?"

"Maybe. Just let it go and the truth of the conditioned mind will just bubble up from inside of you."

"Okay, all I know is I just want to be special to someone." She hesitates for a moment then looks at me. Her eyes nearly pop out of their sockets in recognition. "I'm not special. The voice said, 'I'm not special.'"

"It's interesting how many of my female clients count the Viagra pills before their husbands or boyfriends go out of town," I observe.

116

She gives me a quizzical look and then almost shouts. "Oh, I'm insecure!" Her face relaxes and an expression of joy and recognition passes over her.

She looks at me as if a tremendous weight has been lifted off her shoulders and says, "Thank you. Oh, thank you. Now I see what's behind it all. This is all about my insecurity."

Yes, it's about insecurity, I observe to myself. The ego-mind always wants to change the subject. So we argue about sex, or money, or housework, or too much work. But these are red herrings. The conversation sounds like it's about some external circumstance, but it never is. The problem is not money, or sex, or your mother-in-law. It's about the emotions. It's about our pain. Most of the conversations we have with one another are about our pain. But the pain is never mentioned. This often happens because we don't know the pain. And yet in our not knowing we are secretly idolizing the pain. We worship our pain by refusing to acknowledge it, and at the same time we're building and shoring up our elaborate defense of the pain.

Angie makes another comment. "I've been insecure all my life. Oh my lord, I can see where it all comes from now."

"You might share your insight with Pat. He can stop sneaking around at night and finally discover how to love you the way you want to be loved."

"I will, I will. Dear Lord, how interesting. Suddenly I don't care what he downloads from the Internet. I just want him to love me and treat me like I'm special. And even as I'm saying that, I can see that it's okay. I'm not that person anymore."

I look at Angie and caution her. "Be vigilant, the voice will try and trick you into this pattern again. Although it will never have exactly the same power over you, it will try to hijack you. The tendency to be insecure may raise its ugly head. Be ready, watch your thoughts; and if you succumb, explain to Pat what happened so any reaction can be healed in awareness."

"Yes, yes. Oh, my God, I feel like I've been released from some prison."

I watch Angie leave. Witness Thought Therapy™ is certainly powerful. Of course the most powerful part is Witness Consciousness. It's as if the witness or the watcher is the therapist. My job is relatively easy. All I have to do is trigger an association that gets swept into the attractor basin of the limbic system. From there the truth of the matter usually emerges as completely obvious to the watcher. The awareness itself is the transformation. That's not to say that the job is over, but the problem is no longer a mystery. The need to stay vigilant for each thought, even the random ones, is still imperative. But the dedicated person now has the recognition in awareness of long-standing patterns that have remained hidden simply because of their pervasive repetition.

Awakening

Angie's big reaction happened after she had entered deeply into the experience of witnessing. This was fortunate, since she clearly knew two things: First, her reaction was about her and not Pat; second, that she had been hijacked by her ego. Her experience as a watcher gave her an anchor in reality from which she could reel herself back into awareness so we could finish processing the reaction.

To know one's self, to know one's patterns of reactivity, to embrace one's pain – the awareness that comes with that uproots the mastery of the dialogical self. We are no longer its slave. We are the masters, and we finally can look at life with innocent perception like that of a child. When we do, we stop *thinking* life and start *living* life. What a wondrous adventure!

Chapter 14: The Importance of Relationships

> *. . . the special relationship is an attempt to re-enact the past and change it. Imagined slights, remembered pain, past disappointments, perceived injustices and deprivations all enter into the special relationship, which becomes a way in which you seek to restore your wounded self-esteem.*

A Course in Miracles

In his landmark book, *The Power of Now*, Eckhart Tolle says something revolutionary. He says if we acknowledge that relationships are more and more in conflict during these times, why not turn this to our advantage.

> *"So whenever your relationship is not working, whenever it brings out the 'madness' in you and in your partner, be glad. What was unconscious is being brought up to the light. It is an opportunity for salvation."*

So your "ex" was an opportunity for salvation but you missed it. No matter. There's always number two or number three. But why is Tolle saying that bringing to light that which is unconscious is our salvation? The unconscious patterns that emerge to cloud our most intimate relationships with madness are those things that prevent us from discovering our true essence. So every day our most intimate relationships are a road map for where to go deep inside ourselves to see what's emerging that stands between us and truth.

119

"But what if I'm not in a relationship?" someone always asks. That, too, can be the same kind of guide. Ask one simple question and answer it as honestly as possible. If you're not in a relationship, is it because the pain of loneliness is less than the pain of closeness? That would be a question for Unicorns to ask themselves.

Here's a similar question for Lions. Are you worshiping the pain of loneliness? In other words, is being alone consuming you? Is it all you think about? Do you constantly yearn for a partner? This is what's up for you – your constant objection to being alone.

Simply put, a relationship (or lack of one) is a mirror. Instead of complaining that we need a different mirror, we need to take a look and look deeply. What we will see is our own ego-mind—that hurt, angry, fearful five-year-old—staring back at us.

James Finley in his beautiful book, *The Contemplative Heart*, tells the story of the spiritual seeker who sets out to climb the mountain to the ultimate goal of spiritual fulfillment which lies at the top. The climb is long and arduous and there are many trials along the away. Then, just as the seeker nears the top, a mournful cry is heard coming from the valley below. It sounds like the cry of a child in trouble. The seeker's first impulse is to ignore the painful sound, as the end of the climb is so near. But after listening to the echoes of the heartfelt cry, the seeker turns back to retrace all those hard-fought steps of growth and development.

Arriving back at the valley floor, the cries of anguish are even more distinct. But to the seeker's surprise the sound leads to the seeker's own home, the childhood home of the seeker. There, huddled in a corner, is the little child that the seeker was so many years ago. With little else left to do, the seeker comforts and holds the child hoping to heal the woundedness that is the source of the pain. Miraculously in that instant of compassion for self, the seeker is transported back to the top of the mountain and the spiritual search is over.

Too often the search is prompted by our need to get away from our inner pain. We are seeking relief, we want to feel better. But in so doing we build the edifice of our defenses even taller and thicker. When we succumb to our temptation, seeking turns to pride and arrogance; and even in its nicest form, seeking is violence.

Relationships are not something to get over. They are something to get into. We are being given the book on what we are. A relationship is a university called "me." Rather than complain, struggle, and act out, we need to surrender to the process of being taught how to finally come home. Our issues are blockages. Once removed, the blockage reveals a signpost pointing toward truth.

THE UNCONSCIOUS IS NOT UNCONSCIOUS

In chapter three, we talked about the paint on the wall. The mind reminds me in many ways of one of those children's magazines with the camouflaged cover. It looks like a picture of a jungle. There are trees and foliage everywhere. Your goal is to find the monkey in the picture. But try as you might, you can't see the monkey until you shift your orientation and your expectations and . . . *Voilà!* Monkey!

Most everything we want to call unconscious is in fact super-conscious. These patterns are huge, but they have faded into the background and become noise that our perceptual filters keep us from sensing. In fact, with enough persistence, we can adjust our filters and will eventually see what has been hidden. This requires us to be lifted out of the reflexive system of limbic recursion. Once on the outside, we see the subconscious clearly since now there are few perceptual filters.

Tolle refers to "knowing" what is happening in us and our partner. This is a tall order. What he means is becoming aware of having the experience of anger or becoming aware of having the experience of avoidance. But we get defensive so automatically, we don't really even know that we're defending. Since blame is easier than awareness, knowing what's really going on is rare.

THE LION /UNICORN PATTERNS ARE THE DEEPEST OF ALL

When I set out to write this book, I was challenged about how to relate it to my earlier work, *The Dance of the Lion and the Unicorn*. Should *Awakening* be a sequel or should it be written without reference to the earlier book? I chose sort of a middle path. This book turns out not to be a sequel, but it is inextricably linked to my view of *Lions* and *Unicorns*. Why is that the case? The Lion and Unicorn patterns are basic to our nature and our early experiences of nurture. As such they are the most unconscious patterns we carry in the ego-mind. Ironically, they are also the most powerful forces at work in our most intimate relationships. Marriage, quite simply is a ritualistic reenactment of our first social relationship formed at around four years of age, as stated earlier.

I have met many people who view themselves as advanced souls. They meditate, they read all the right books, and they use all the appropriate "New

Age" vocabulary. Yet their relationships are a mess. Their basic message is "I'm a spiritual type of guy or gal, as long as I stay away from my mate." This obviously implies that their partner is the person who is unenlightened.

This is an especially slippery slope for Unicorns. Lions, being the ones who openly express anger, cannot escape the fact that their reactivity is deeply unconscious. Unicorns, on the other hand, can easily hide in their passive defenses and even act out their passive-aggressive hostility since it's not overtly unacceptable socially.

If you assiduously watch your thoughts and find yourself in *witness consciousness*, your motives, and your partner's motives, become crystal clear. To someone witnessing, any form of unconsciousness becomes abundantly clear.

I was recently at a meeting with someone who was deep in her passive defenses. Her act was so slick that it was easy for me to be fooled from time to time. There was a lot of name-dropping of spiritual leaders, authors, and groups. She went out of her way to use all of the right words, to mouth a lot of platitudes about enlightenment, and reference lofty philosophies about the condition of humankind.

After the meeting, I felt as if I'd been slimed. The person with me was a practitioner of witness consciousness. He turned to me and said, "She is really deep in her own shit, isn't she?" That pretty much summed it up. She was a lovely person with a lot of knowledge, trying very hard to be awakened without leaving the mind or her identification with thought. As such she justified her passive strategies, sanctified her passive defenses, and put on a game face of depth. My heart cried out for a way to reach her, to free her from her ego-mind. But I knew she must free herself.

But let's not let the Lions off of the hook so easily. They just don't tend to hide their issues in false spirituality. Unicorns will hide in sheep's clothing. Lions are just busy killing all the sheep.

The bottom line is that the relationship itself is the mirror in which we need to see what we need to see about ourselves. Paradoxically, we need to see very little about our partner except the emotional pain that they hold deep inside. Once we glimpse that, we know intuitively how to meet their needs. No, we don't need to become experts on them. Expertise is reserved for ourselves. And the thing we need to see more than anything else about ourselves keeps causing us to react in the relationship.

The Lion/Unicorn model is a rich source of process maps to guide us to look at exactly what we're doing and how we're doing it. The *content* of the problem in any relationship is not particularly useful from a personal-growth point of view. But the *process* is of extreme value. The question is not *why*.

The question is *how*. To a large extent, the Lion/Unicorn model answers this *how*. *How* invariably reveals the way the mind works—which is the prison in which we are stuck.

Surrender to What Is

The literature on enlightenment and self-realization is rife with the advice to surrender to *what is*. Why should we do this? What does this surrender really mean? And what do relationships have to do with it?

First we must look at the concept of "what is." To do this, I would like to introduce an almost religious slant to my ideas at this point. It's not that I'm particularly religious, I'm not. Most religion is organized for the advancement of the ego and has nothing to do with truth or what is actually divine. And that includes eastern religion as well. That being said, I want to use religious language since I think that will very simply convey something astonishing in the clearest terms.

Consider the following question that I ask many when we get to this point in the discovery of truth. Where is God? The answer I normally get is something like this: He is everywhere. He is here. Everywhere we go, He is there. The answer comes across as if God is a visitor who has the divine quality of making an invisible appearance wherever. So you and I live our lives and God is an invisible voyeur, an eavesdropper who, like Santa Claus, is going to decide who is naughty and who is nice. If you're naughty, you'll go to hell where you'll be fried and fricasseed for all eternity. If you're good, you'll go to heaven and live in one of the "many mansions" that Jesus is preparing for us (John 4:12). You may want a room with a view or one overlooking the garden. On your way, God may trip you up, kill you, make you sick, or grind you into powder for no apparent reason.

To clear up the obvious problem with this line of reasoning, let's consider the three generally accepted characteristics of God: Omniscience (all-knowing), Omnipotence (all-powerful), and Omnipresence (all-present). What does it mean to be all present? It means ubiquitous, being everywhere at the same time. Omnipresent means infinitely present. By logical extension, then, there is nothing but God. You are God, the desk is God, and the space between molecules is God. We are bathed in Divine Essence, what the Apostle Paul called the Spirit of God (Romans 8:9). There is nothing but God.

God is not everywhere as if he is an infinitely irritating visitor. God is everywhere in such a way that the Presence of God crowds out the possibility of anything else being in existence.

But how can this be? What about all the evil in the world? What's to be done with the people I don't agree with? This is like Oberon, the king of the fairies, disputing Shakespeare's plotting in *A Midsummer Night's Dream*. It is a play within a play, a dream. Can you imagine the arrogance of Oberon complaining to Shakespeare that he should be nicer to his characters? We will look into this more later.

In any event, the idea is that everything is God. If that's the case, you are the Divine Expression and so is your spouse. So your mate, the present moment, your life situation, and the party that controls Congress are all the divine expression. If the present is God why do we always say NO!? We have our objections to just about everything. Sure, everything is God unless we happen to disagree.

I heard the awakened teacher, Leonard Jacobson, say that the promise of future fulfillment is the trick of the ego. In our arrogance we think we have a better idea. We object, complain, and say, "God, I'm waiting for a better moment than the one you're giving me right now, okay?" So we have our ego-minds firmly planted in the anticipated future rather than the Divine Present. If we said yes instead of no, how different would our lives be!

Nowhere does our lack of acceptance and our resistance to "what is" become more apparent than in our relationships. We focus on our partner's need to change, to make us happy, and to meet our needs. We blame and attack, we criticize and gossip. We talk behind their backs about their weaknesses. We have no shame. We will even use our children as weapons against them. The evil and violence we visit on our partners knows no bounds.

You might be saying that I'm a little over the top. Remember, I'm a marriage counselor. I watch the horror of disintegrating relationships. I see what people do to one another in the name of being right. I've seen what happens to their children. They are used as pawns in a game of retribution and self-justification.

Before we go too deep into the darkness of human depravity, let me tell you a story. One Sunday I was visiting a church. I was to do a relationships workshop the next week, and was there to promote the event.

The female minister told the following story that has stayed in my heart ever since. She reminisced that many years ago, a particular Saturday night was like most nights and certainly most Saturday nights. Her husband was passed out drunk on the sofa. There she was abandoned, alone, and distraught. What could she do? She cried out to God. Why was she being punished? Why was her husband such a loser? Woe is me! She was angry and upset. This had been going on for years and she wasn't sure how much longer she could put up with it.

Being a minister, she was obligated to pray about it. In the prayer of her misery, a thought came to her. If her husband changed, and loved her the way she wanted to be loved, what kind of wife would she be in the marriage? Well, she thought, she would be loving, and compassionate, and caring, and all those things she knew were the best things to do in a marriage.

Suddenly, her heart was convicted. She was supposed to be doing those things anyway! She saw that in her resistance to *what is*, she was saying *no* to God. She had become angry and bitter and had refused her love to her husband. She saw how she retaliated by judging him, castigating him, and hating him. That moment she vowed never to fall into that trap again, and she set out to turn herself around no matter how he behaved.

This produced a miracle and the upshot was that he got up off the couch (figuratively and literally) and went to AA. She finished the story by saying he had been sober for fourteen years and they were more in love than ever.

This story shows so many things. Our resistance and objections act as a constraint in the relationship. It becomes the glue that holds everything in place. Our willingness to accept things as they are and to accept our partner exactly as she or he is releases the bonds and lets change come into our lives.

This is not to say that loving what is and acceptance mean we never get a divorce, we never leave when we're being abused, or we tolerate unsafe behavior. But it does mean that *hate* is not a part of *right action*. If we truly watch our thoughts, there is no reaction. The right action for the situation emerges from within us without the need for retaliation or defending.

If God is infinitely present, then the relationship is Divine. We are being held in a crucible called "relationship" for our learning and enlightenment. If we will learn to say "yes" to the Divinity of the present and its manifestation in our lives, we will solve a great mystery concerning our true identity.

Taking ownership of everything that comes from the mind is difficult for everyone. Even students of meditation that have spent years in Eastern practices want to blame the other person in a conflict. We all want to retaliate, we want to be right, we don't want to see our part.

A well known Eastern saying sums up the problem with relationships. "All instruction is but a finger pointing to the moon. He whose gaze is fixed upon the pointer will never see beyond. Let him even catch sight of the moon, still he cannot see its beauty." A relationship is a pointer. It points to Truth. But when our gaze is fixed on the finger, we won't recognize the Truth to which the finger points.

Chapter 15: The Destruction of "me"

Arranging thought in the order of value, the "I"-thought is the all important thought. Personality-idea or thought is also the root or stem of all other thoughts, since each idea or thought arises only as someone's thought and is not known to exist independently of the ego.

Ramana Maharshi

Jerry has been coming to me for some time. He has been a great student of witnessing. I clearly remember the first night he and his wife came in. He was obviously scared and frustrated. His wife was done. She wanted a divorce. She was obviously the Unicorn in the relationship. Having reached her saturation of "overwhelm," she didn't know what else to do but opt out. Living with the constant fear of his angry outbursts and his heavy drinking was bad enough. But like a true Unicorn, she had allowed it to build and build to the point where she felt she had no option but to end the relationship.

Jerry had come from an abusive childhood that had left its marks on his thinking. He was not well educated and it became immediately apparent that he struggled with attention deficit disorder. He worked an extremely high-pressure job. By the time he came home at night, I speculated, he had no internal resources left to handle his emotions.

"So Jerry, how goes it?"

"It goes well. You know, this thought-watching thing is without a doubt the biggest idea ever. When I first came in to see you, I would never have even guessed that there was an option about thoughts. I just automatically took them on. The concept that I didn't have to do that never would have occurred to me."

Jerry was a surprise to me. I've learned never to judge whether a person is ready for the work of separating themselves from their identification with thought. Had I gone with the speculation of my mind at the time, I would have guessed that Jerry just didn't have the capacity to become detached from the drama. A tough background sometimes makes doing any insight work virtually impossible. The beauty of Witness Thought Therapy™ is that it is not an assault on the defenses, so its form of insight can come very easily.

Jerry took to it immediately. It made perfect sense to him and he grabbed hold of it in the first session. He came in the next week a new man.

"Once you break the ties of the identified thinker, life does take on a whole new meaning doesn't it? By the way, how's the wife?"

"The thing I notice is that as long as I stay in awareness, life takes on a flow. I can feel a joy in living like I've never felt before. My wife? Tina doesn't know what to make of me. I'm not the same person who came in here ten weeks ago. Thanks a lot."

"Is she still insisting on a divorce?"

"Oh yeah, but not with the same energy. She's just stubborn and doesn't want to admit that I've changed. But I'm in a very different place with all this now. If she should go ahead with that, it's okay. I don't have to make it a drama. It will be hard, but I'll just relax into it and let go of any thoughts that come along to try and convince me otherwise. But honestly, I don't think that will happen."

It feels good to me to see how Jerry's life has changed. He is literally a different person from the guy I met a few weeks ago. He looks relaxed, he's more articulate, and he seems much more present in the room with me.

"You know, Jerry; it seems that this may be your last session with me. The witness inside of you can do the rest."

"I've been thinking about that. I don't want to stop just yet, although I do want to join one of your support groups. I can see without a regular reminder that I might be inclined to think I've got it and drift back into my old habits."

"Yes, that would be a wise decision. You don't know how much I think about the people who have come here, entered into witness consciousness, and just left. I hope they're getting fed and supported somewhere. This is a doorway, not a destination."

Jerry shifts in his chair and looks like he's searching for words. "You know, that doorway thing. I wanted to ask you about that. Now that I'm the watcher, what's next?"

"Well, let me demonstrate. You know how to watch your thoughts, right?"

"Yep."

"Okay, just remain in witness consciousness and watch. As you watch, ask yourself this question: Who is watching?"

Jerry seems in deep concentration. He looks up at me and says, "Me. I'm watching."

"Look again," I urge. "Ask the question, 'who is this *me* watching?' and use awareness to look deeply inside. What do you see?"

There is silence in the room as Jerry looks inside himself. "Nothing, there's nothing there. Is that what I was supposed to see?" He looks at me with question marks in his eyes.

"Jerry, do you want to try something radical?"

Jerry nods and I continue, "Okay, I want you to tell me the one thing you absolutely know for sure in this moment." I hold up my cell phone. "How can you prove that this cell phone exists in something you and I might call reality?"

Jerry looks at me like I've just lost my marbles. "Please, let's just play with this for a moment. Don't run screaming from the room just yet."

"Okay doc, but you're freaking me out a little here."

"Let me take a step back." I hold up my cell phone again. "Tell me scientifically, how do you know that this is a cell phone?"

Jerry understands the question and dives into the answer. "Let's see. The nerves in your eyes and hands send signals to the brain. Then the brain compares that input to learned information from the past and a match is formed. That's how we know it's a cell phone."

"Right, but we're not really experiencing the cell phone, are we?"

He looks at me funny for a moment and then suddenly his eyes light up. "Oh my God, we're not having a real experience of the cell phone. It's nerve impulses and brain chemicals and stuff."

"How right you are. We're not having a direct experience of anything. What we call reality is nothing more than a representation happening in the brain. It's electrical, it's holographic, and it is nothing more than an appearance in our awareness."

"I see. That much I understand. I get it."

"Okay, now back to my original question. Knowing what we know, what is the one thing that you can prove? It is undeniable."

"Well, since I have no direct experience of anything, but I am having an experience of something, I guess the one thing that's real for certain is that I'm having some kind of experience. Is that it?"

"You're on the right track. But let's take away the experience for a moment. Now what are you left with?"

Jerry thinks for a moment and then nearly shouts, "I exist! Awareness that I exist!"

"Yes, that's it. The one thing that's undeniable is that there is 'being'ness, or 'am'ness or 'is'ness. There is existence. Another way we might speak of it is as the presence of awareness, or the awareness of presence – take your pick."

There is a silence in the room. There is awareness. There is presence. The stillness of the silence seems to go on forever.

Jerry looks at me and says, "Wait a minute. Wait just a minute. What about me? Where am I in all this 'am'ness?"

"Well, that's where the doorway of witness consciousness leads. Who is watching? There is no who. There is only *watching*. There is only awareness. Prove it for yourself. Go look. Keep looking until you discover who or what is looking."

"I mean what about my personality? Are you telling me that I have some kind of personality disorder?"

"An awakened teacher by the name of Katie Davis was once asked that question. You know what she said?"

Jerry's eyes are big. "No," he whispers.

She said, "Yes, the personality is a disorder."

#

It has been many weeks since I've seen Pat and Angie. As they enter my office and settle in, I'm anxious to get caught up on their lives.

Angie is the first to speak; but as she does, I notice Pat has a new energy in his presence. Angie says, "I just want to thank you for dealing with me the other week. I know it must have been uncomfortable for you to see me in that state."

"You know how much I love you guys. I'll go through it if you will. But you have to want it more than I want it for you. That's my only condition."

"Well, I was more than a little embarrassed to find that all of my fussing and fighting was really about my own insecurity. But I went home and apologized to Pat for my behavior. I told him he can download whatever, as long as he shows he loves me."

Pat pipes up, "Actually, the entire incident has helped me, too. When I understood what Angie had discovered, I redoubled my efforts at watching my thoughts. I was especially curious to see what my mind was doing around porn. I found out the damndest thing. I'm embarrassed about my sexuality."

"Yes, and we had a long talk about it, too." Angie smiled. "I think I understand men better since we talked. But boy, our sex life has been off the scale since then."

"Ironically," Pat says, "Angie had wanted a little more adventure and variety in our sex life, but I was too embarrassed to go there."

"And I was so wound up in my jealousy and insecurity, I thought that anything Pat considered adventuresome was somehow a putdown or a threat to me. Typical Lion stuff—ha."

I smiled. "Great, so now you're looking at this aspect of your life together through the lens of compassion and respect for the other person. This is wonderful to hear."

Angie says, "Anyway, we wanted to come in for one last session to let you know what's going on and how we've resolved things."

"By the way," Pat says, "this won't be the last you see of us. We're going to be regulars at the support groups. I never want to lose the gains we've made. And I hope we can share our successes with others."

I lean back feeling very satisfied. I couldn't ask for more. "There are so many people out there stuck in their heads. Awakening is such a gift. We must do everything we can to tell the world."

"Yes, and I personally can testify to the axiom you keep quoting, that reactions tell us nothing about the other person, they only tell us about ourselves," interjects Angie.

Pat has something on his mind. "Before we let you go and move on to whatever, there's still something missing for me. Remember when I came in after having that somewhat mystical experience of peace?"

"Of course."

"I feel like there's something more, or something I'm not getting. I mean, I felt the bliss and I wanted so to get back to it. You showed me how to move into witness consciousness and how to be the watcher. But I still feel like there's more. I watch my thoughts. I'm so good at it that I rarely get lost in thought anymore. I really do have a very detached view of anything that thought might represent. I live in this sort of peaceful gray area. I know I am in the world, but not of the world. My question is, does this lead to something? Or is this it?"

Angie nods and says, "I guess my question is the same. I'm also experiencing that sense of other, of being separated from the activity of the mind. So if I'm other than my thoughts, if I'm watching instead of identifying, who am I? What am I supposed to do with my life? Remember, you told us you left something out of that chart."

This is a fundamental question that Pat and Angie have asked. But there's no way to answer it directly that will satisfy the mind. So I must go at it indirectly. It's not that the truth needs to be discovered. The truth is enormous, but as with our mind patterns, we're so used to it being there that we don't distinguish it. To me it's like being at a costume party. Everyone is wearing a mask, wondering how to discover their true self.

"I'd like to go at this in a little different fashion, if that's okay. I want to demonstrate what you are not. The ultimate reality of who you are will not emerge until what's false is ripped away."

"Fire away," says Angie. Pat nods his agreement.

"Ok, so you both know very well how to watch your thoughts, correct?"

"Correct."

"So what I want you to do is to go inside and silently repeat to yourselves 'My name is Pat' or 'My name is Angie.' Do it over and over again. While you're doing it, see if you can notice the feeling of *me* that goes along with the recognition of your internal voice."

Pat looks at Angie and then at me. "I'm not sure I understand. We're supposed to repeat our names?"

"Right. Say, 'My name is Pat' over and over again."

"Okay?"

"Now you know that internal voice is *your* internal voice, right? It's not Angie's voice. It's your voice."

"Got it. So. . .?"

"As you say your name with that voice, notice the feeling of recognition that goes along with hearing the voice say your name. In other words, it's a feeling of, 'Hey, that's my voice saying my name.' It's a feeling of 'me.' Do you get it?" I see that Pat and Angie are a little confused.

"Just do it. While you do it, use your awareness of your mind and watch the sensations that come with the internal voice. You will eventually notice a totally obvious sensation, feeling, recognition, call it what you will, that is the feeling of your distinct internal voice. It's *me, me* talking in my head."

Angie mumbles, "It's me talking in my head." And I watch her go inside and start the monologue of naming. In a few seconds she looks at me. "Of course, I get it. There's a *me* feeling that goes with the voice. Sort of a *me* identification."

"Right. How about you, Pat?"

"I'm pretty sure I understand. Yes, there is a distinct *me*. As if it's *me* talking. I mean, who else would it be?"

"Yes, it's the sensation of who's talking—the identified talker, if you will. It's like I asked you Whose car is that? and you said It's mine. There's a *me* feeling that goes with the thought 'my car.'"

"Oh, that's it. I can see it now."

I look at both of them just to check in and make sure they're on the same page with me. "Okay, step two. As you repeat your name and feel that *me* feeling, go look at it with your awareness as if it's a thought just like any other thought. So the purpose of repeating your name is to bring up the feeling of the identified 'me.' Look at that *me* and see what happens. Go into witness consciousness and look. Tell me what happens."

Angie and Pat both go silent for a few minutes. Finally, Angie looks up and says, "It goes away. Dear lord!"

Pat looks at Angie. "You too? I thought I was losing my mind. The feeling of *me* kept going away when I looked at it. I thought maybe I wasn't doing it right."

"So let's recap here. When you're witnessing your thoughts they go away, disappear, stop, however you want to describe it. Now when you witness the little *me* in the head, it goes away in the same fashion. When we look at the mind with awareness, it stops. Thoughts stop, the personality disappears, and the little self evaporates." I finish with a grin.

Pat and Angie are still a little stunned. Pat asks, "Where does it come from? If it's really not there when you look, where does it come from?"

Angie puts up her hand as if to say "Whoa." "Pat, I don't mean to interrupt. But before we go on to that, I have a question. Is that okay?"

Pat gestures for her to go ahead.

She turns to me. "So what we have here is a situation where awareness of the process of thought stops thought. We know that. When we observe ourselves experiencing thought, the mind stops, and the thought evaporates. Okay, so now what you're telling me is that when I observe myself, 'I' go away? This raises all kinds of questions as to who is the observer, not to mention who the hell am I."

"Let me put this in a little better perspective for you," I begin. "For years the literature of enlightenment has talked about the 'I-thought' which is essentially the same concept as the 'false self.' So the 'I-thought' or feeling of 'me' is like a thought that wraps itself around every other thought. But just like thought-identification, *me* identification is an illusion. When you watch thought, it disappears revealing the feeling of a 'me' who is the thinker. When you watch the thinker – *me*, it disappears revealing just the mind. When you look at the mind – well, you get the idea."

Angie looks at me and says, "Can you repeat that?"

I go the white board and draw a diagram that looks like this:

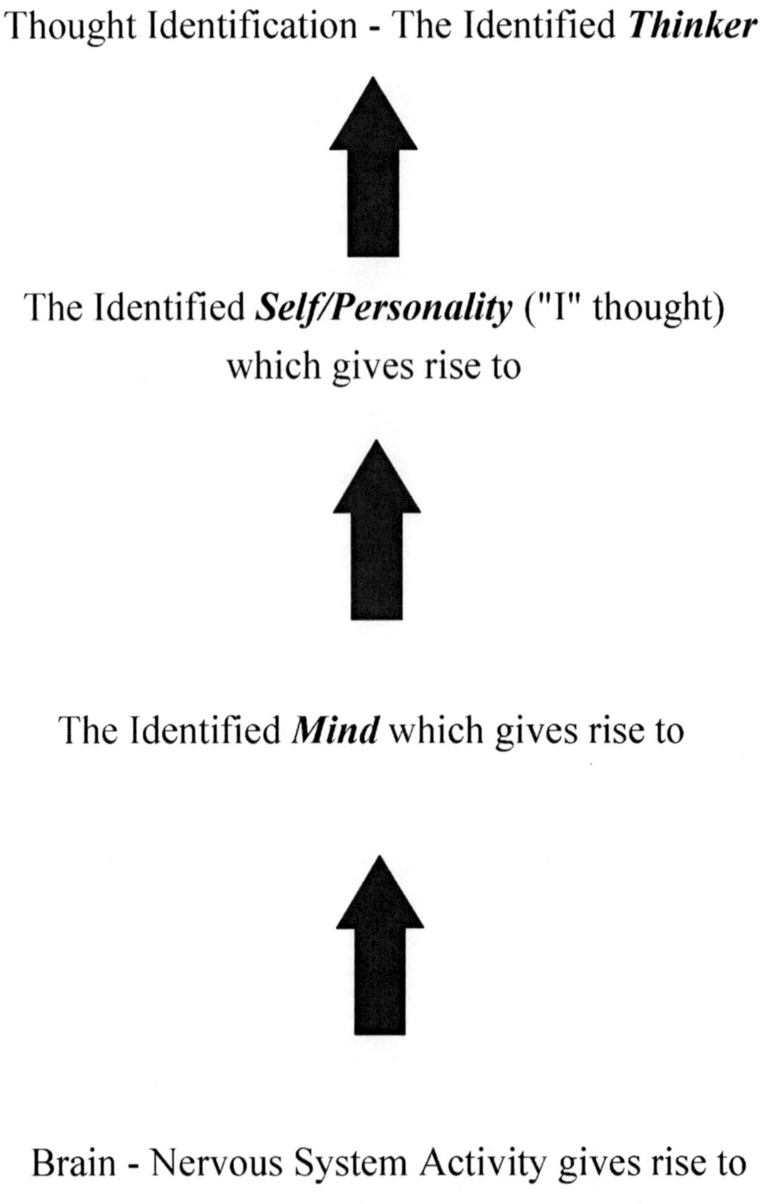

Thought Identification - The Identified *Thinker*

The Identified *Self/Personality* ("I" thought) which gives rise to

The Identified *Mind* which gives rise to

Brain - Nervous System Activity gives rise to

Figure 15-1 The false identification of humankind

"What this says is that when we identify with mental activity associated with the brain and nervous system, we mistakenly become the 'identified mind.' Or put simply, we think we have a *mind*. And also, we mistakenly identify with the body. The mind identification leads to 'self'-identification or the false assumption that this mind activity must belong to a *me*. This is the 'I-thought.' Before you know it, the little self or *me* in the head thinks that thoughts are its thoughts and the *identified thinker* is born. This is all false identification that camouflages who or what we really are."

Pat speaks up as he is furiously copying my diagram on a piece of paper. "Man, I'm going to have to think about this for a while. I feel like I'm gagging on a piece of steak that was too big."

Angie has been studying the diagram and speaks in a thoughtful voice. "What you're saying is that *the entire framework or reference point of our individual lives is based on false identification.* So who are we?"

"Go inside and look," I urge. "Ask yourself, If there's no 'me' or personality, what's left? If there is witnessing, where is the witness? Who is the watcher? But wait, we just destroyed the individual as the watcher. So there can only be *watching*. What is this *watching?*"

"God?" asks Angie.

"Essentially, yes. Of course 'God' is only a verbal representation of something that's un-manifested and inconceivable, not to mention ineffable. But yes. And since we've speculated that this 'presence of awareness' takes up residence in the prefrontal lobes, let me give you a diagram to contemplate."

I go to the white board and erase the previous diagram and replace it with a sketch that looks like this:

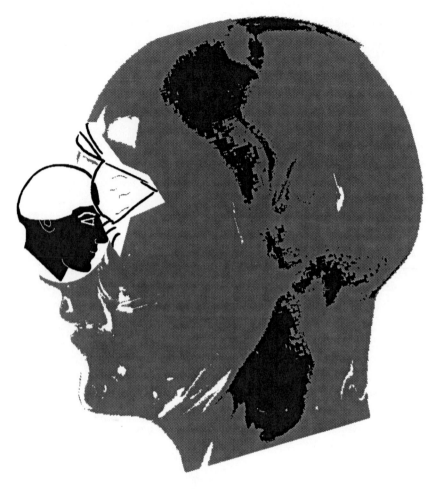

Figure 15-2 The Prefrontal lobes as the eye of the "I"

"Good, God, that drawing is absolutely creepy!" shouts Angie.

"Sorry, I'm not a gifted artist."

Meanwhile Pat has been studying my drawing for a minute or two. "Is this what they call "self-realization" or "enlightenment?" God looking through us at the world?"

"Realizing the Self is to realize that the world, the physical, manifested universe, is the Self of God."

Before Pat and Angie start to leave I pull a book from the shelf and read this quote:

The eye through which I see God is the same eye through which God sees me; my eye and God's eye are one eye, one seeing, one knowing, one love.

Meister Eckhart

"That is kind of what I was trying to portray in my sketch. That quote from Meister Eckhart reminds me of another quote."

I rummage around my book case and pull out *A Course in Miracles.* "Lesson thirty says this, 'God is in everything I see because God is in my mind.'"

Angie looks at me and asks, "So what are we supposed to do to experience ourselves as one eye?"

"There is no doing. It's a matter of orientation. The 'one eye' reality has always been there. We just ignore it. Think of it this way. The reason that thoughts stop when we turn our awareness to them – the reason the voice in our head goes silent is because the brain can't do two things at once. We can't talk to ourselves and pay attention at the same time. We literally must leave the present moment when we go into our heads to identify with thought.

As you have just seen, we have to go into our heads to experience a 'self' as the owner of those thoughts or the 'doer.' But the Divine Essence of life is right here right now. So in order to experience a separate person, a little me in the head, we must leave the Divine Essence of life and construct a mental world of a conceptual 'me' having thoughts and doing things in the world.

So the answer is simply to pay attention. Pay attention to thought, pay attention to the construction of the personality or self, and finally pay attention to what is right in front of us. When we do that, we open to the possibility that my eye and God's eye are one. And the seeing merges into that with is seen as the unity of the Divine."

Chapter 16: Levels of Consciousness

Where is the so called self located? I have searched long and hard for a self and haven't found it anywhere. It appears to not be lost, but rather to never have been there to begin with. The concept of self occurs as part of every thought.

Steven Harrison

In the last chapter we saw the trap into which humankind has fallen. It is a trap of false identification. Surrounded and pervaded by the Divine Manifestation, we choose to identify with our bodies, our sensations, and our mental activity. We are the identified body, mind, and thinker. We do not live life, we think life. The limbic system, ego-mind, carnal nature, call it what you will, has tricked us into the belief that as long as we stay in our heads, we will outlive God—which is ironic because fundamentally all that is, is God. There is no *we*. Oh! Yes, there appear to be individual expressions of the divine, but there are no individuals. So we are left with the choice of being either an expression or an ego. That makes the decision easy! We are one; there is unity, not duality and separateness. Yet we live in the tortured dream state of our own drama and struggle.

Jesus said, ". . . and I have given them the *doxa* which you gave to me, so that they may be one, just as we are one." *Doxa* is something that enables humans to all be one. *Doxa* is a Greek word that is translated as *glory*. Originally it meant common opinion or common belief. Later it came to mean high opinion or honor. By extension it means recognition or realization. But there is no direct meaning in English. It is a combination of magnificence, enlightenment, grace, praise, and glory. To sum this up – Self-realization. When we realize the Self, we immediately see the unity of the physical manifestation.

THE PERSONALITY

What then is the personality? It is what makes us an individual. Being an individual runs counter to what we just said. So what does make us an individual? There are two things that combine to make up this so-called personality: our inborn traits and our conditioning. Personality is thought to be heavily influenced by childhood development. Childhood development encapsulates our earliest relationships and experiences.

As humans, we experience constantly shifting roles. Sometimes we are the victim and play the role of the pain-filled child. Sometimes we avoid or defend – attack or escape. More often we play the role of being reasonable, urbane, and knowledgeable. Our inborn traits are socialized. We become sophisticated, adept at the finer points of social intercourse.

Our family role is re-enacted in our homes and marriages. The roles learned in an alcoholic family are well-known. We all come out of the family of origin with an adaptive role.

Social scientists wrap this all up into a large field of study called "Personality Theory." Do you know why it's called a theory? Because it's not real, or tangible. The personality cannot be found. We all have various acts we put on. Invariably we love our act. It's called a personality.

So if it's not real, what is it? What we call personality is nothing more than a series of patterns of responses wrapped around goal-directed emotional states that are driven by the limbic system. We take the mosaic of the mind stuff that becomes what we call social interaction and character traits and call it "my personality." It is nothing more than an amalgamation of limbic stances that serves us in presenting the ego to the world.

This is not to say it's bad. But like the mind itself, this amorphous thing we call a personality is nothing more than our act, persona, or mask that has wrapped itself around our inborn traits in an alchemy of identification that becomes what we call "me." It's supposed to be a tool we use to get along in the world. You pick it up and use it. One person has a clever wit. Another has a delightful giggle. What was supposed to be a way of identifying a mind-body unit belonging to Sam or Bill or Linda has become an obsessive, self-indulgent, and tedious set of ego-states designed to delight the crowd.

The personality is nothing more than emotionally instigated behavior patterns that have the goal of promoting our self-interest and survival. It includes the dialogical self and its constantly shifting positionality. This is wrapped with a decorative ribbon of identification called the "I" thought which constantly reminds us that this act is *my* act – this is "me." The personality can be summed up in the singing words of Bugs Bunny from the 1950s show, *"What's up Doc?"*

> *Oh, we're the boys of the chorus / We hope you like our show /*
> *We know you're rooting for us / But now we have to go!*
> *We've got our hat. We've got our cane, and we're dancin'.*

YOU ARE NOT THE "DOER"

You probably don't realize it, but the argument over free will and life being predestined has largely been settled. In 1983, a psychological researcher by the name of Benjamin Libet and some colleagues at the University of California San Francisco did a landmark experiment. They measured the brain and how it functioned during a task that allowed for choice. What they found was that the signals in the motor cortex that initiate action actually start .5 seconds before we become aware that we have "decided" to act. My wife has a favorite phrase for these kinds of things. She calls them "spookynesses."

What this means is very simple. We don't have a choice in what we do. We are going to do whatever it is in the script that says we will do what we do. In other words, we are not the *doer* of life. *Life is doing us.* Life just happens. There is no egoic control of anything. This personality that we think we are is doing nothing.

What is happening is that as life happens, the ego-mind (limbic system) comes in within a half second to take credit for it. Try this experiment. Assuming you are reading this sitting down, predict with accuracy the exact instant that you will get out of your chair or reach for a drink or blow your nose. If you are honest, you will find that action just happens. Oh yes, a thought might occur to you that you're having an itch on your butt, but the exact instant you reach back there cannot be known by the conscious mind. Sure enough the ego will come in later with a sigh of relief and say, "Oh, I'm glad I decided to do that. I feel much better."

I have to admit that Libet and company have had their detractors. Other scientists have come up with elaborate rationalizations as to why what Libet proved was not that we don't have free will. It must be something else. It is

Awakening

hard for our egos to admit that we're not in control, that life is living us not the other way around.

BACK IN THE BOWL

In the 1984 movie *All of Me,* Lily Tomlin dies and her soul goes into a bowl which promptly falls out of a window and onto/into Steve Martin. Her soul is transferred to him and for the rest of the movie he tries to get her soul "back in the bowl."

You may feel a little like this has happened to you. I just took everything you knew to be true about yourself and basically put it into a bowl and threw it out the window. I've said that the mind is nothing but false identification with brain activity. I've said that the self/me/personality is false identification with mind stuff. And I've said that the life we think we live is false since it is based on identification with thinking.

The natural question is if I am not what I identify myself to be, who or what am I? Descartes was dead wrong when he said, "I think, therefore I am." He should have said, "I am the awareness of thinking." Stop reading right now and ask yourself this question. What is the container of your experience? Is it the mind? Is it thought? Is it the "self?" No! It is awareness, "being"ness, "is"ness, presence. The presence of awareness is the bowl that contains the world. The one thing we're all sure of is that we exist. It is this "existingness" that engulfs the mind and body.

LEVELS OF CONSCIOUSNESS

Imagine you are reading a novel. In the novel a character is struggling with spiritual growth and awakening. From the viewpoint of the character, there is a choice to be made; there is effort to be put in place. From the reader's standpoint, it's obvious that there's no choice; the character's actions are predetermined. But until the character wakes up and realizes the truth of the novel, the illusion of choice is very real. This is the situation in which we find ourselves. Spiritual teacher Richard Rose said two things that highlight our situation: "You have to fight like hell to find out there's nothing to fight like hell for" and "We don't have free will but we must act as if we did."

This book is written from the standpoint of the character in the novel, as it does no good to tell someone that everything is predestined. You can't sit with a drink in your hand and wait for enlightenment to occur. Some effort must be made even if the effort is an illusion. Once the Self is fully realized, it becomes obvious that no effort was necessary. It is a paradox. Unfortunately, there are too many "teachers" who tell us there is nothing we can do, but don't give us an appropriate way of integrating non-doing. *Seeing* what is false is this non-doing. Seeing comes from awareness. Doing comes from the ego-mind.

To the reader of the novel, clearly there are no levels of consciousness to be achieved, attained, or otherwise appropriated. But to the character, there is a definite progression of sorts. The chart below is an attempt at summarizing this.

Experience	State	Label
Awareness with no 'self" reference point	Isness, Amness, pure being	The Self, Christ, Buddha Mind
Awareness of the Thinker as Other	Detachment from the thinker	Witness consciousness
Seeing unconsciousness	Awareness of ego patterns	Self-observation
The content of thought	I am my thoughts	The identified thinker

Table 16-1 Levels of consciousness

The lowest level of consciousness is that of *identification*. We identify with our body, mind, personality, and our conditioned thoughts. Every thought is imbibed and processed into a progression that changes the body and puts us into a state of readiness. The mind-body complex produces a steady stream of thoughts, most of which are the dialogical self, getting us ready for the next anticipated moment. We exist in a state of belief that these thoughts are *our thoughts*, that we must give them authority over us, and that there is legitimacy to their existence since they are our thoughts. Our experience of life is limited to the content of thought at this level of consciousness. It is not a happy place. It is an "outer darkness filled with tears and the gnashing of teeth."

One can only hope to get some insight into one's self. This *self* is usually not a pretty picture. But it is necessary in finding the truth of who we really are to bust our own act. This is called *self-observation*, by means of which we can have the experiences of seeing ourselves for the first time. We see how unconscious we are and begin to become aware of ego patterns. Unfortunately these patterns don't make us look good. The self-observer discovers that he or she is arrogant, hostile, attacking, and self-promoting. We come face to face with our need to be right and to survive at everyone else's expense. And if the experience of self-observation is complete enough, we get a bird's-eye view of how we have screwed up our children with our ego games.

Self-observation brings with it a humility that is refreshing and opens the door to further growth. It's a crack in the ego. Often times, since the truth within us has such power, we may have mystical experiences, sensations of peace, bliss, and even out-of-body experiences. Please remember that self-discovery has little to do with peak or other sensate experiences.

A refinement of self-observation is *witnessing* thought. Even though it is still observation, it's a giant leap that not only affects what is observed, but transports the aspirant to a new level of consciousness. *Witness consciousness* is the first stage of true dis-identification and detachment from the world of the thinker, which is the world of illusion. There is now distance between the watcher and the thinker and a knowing that thoughts are not commands, but mere passing clouds in the sky of the mind.

With *witness consciousness*, perception is freed up to allow the watcher to see through the conditioned mind and into the heart of the matter. Motives become clear. The pain behind reactivity is seen. One client, mentioned in chapter 11, described it as: "It's as if I've been looking through just one small pane of a window. Now I can see through all the panes."

Here is the formal description that I use in my support groups to describe witness consciousness:

> Awakening is waking up from the daytime dream and realizing that who you thought you were is not limited to thought, emotion or form. A detachment occurs, resulting in the witnessing of thought and the internal voice of the conditioned mind.
>
> Mark invites you to recognize the preciousness of Being and to directly experience the illusion of suffering due to misidentification with and the attachment to conditioned thought. The portal is attention and alertness to this moment, free of an imaginary past and free from the projection and delusion of the future. Life is none other than here and now.

Even though awakening to witness consciousness is nothing short of a rebirth, there is a problem. The witness, the identified personality doing the witnessing, does not exist. It is only after the ego collapses and the separation of witness and that which is witnessed evaporates that we finally awaken to the non-dual reality of life. This is Self-realization with a big "S." Reality is experienced as being the reader of the novel, rather than one of its characters. Life no longer surrounds us. It implodes because the story of life and the world which contains it is itself contained within the Self. This is pure being, isness, livingness – with no reference to a little "me" in the head that is a *doer* of the living.

AWAKENING VS. SELF-REALIZATION

Many people use these terms interchangeably. I do not. This didn't come to me as a divine revelation, but I think it's helpful to label the experiences I have observed in a useful way to act as pointers. Awakening is a definite shift that happens when a person gets a glimpse of truth. In some cases, this comes with the first observation of the ego-mind and our programmed patterns. There is sometimes a shift to an outside perspective. This shatters the ego a little and the truth comes pouring forth for a short time. Usually the person is filled with peace and bliss. Sometimes these awakening experiences are spontaneous. More often they accompany a person's decision that their awful life can no longer go on and something must be done. This recognition triggers a crack in the ego which produces an awakening.

My evangelical friends will not like my next comment, but it fits right in here. When people ask "Jesus" into their lives as a personal savior, this also is a crack in the ego in much the same fashion as mentioned above. And as with any form of surrender, Truth is ready with its anointing.

So in those rare moments of despair and surrender, people often have the experience of their true essence. This is fulfilling and leaves an unquenchable thirst for more after the experience has receded.

I believe strongly that The Awakening can be induced. This is what thought-watching is all about. The entry into witness consciousness that happens as a result of observing the experience of thought produces this same awakening. This usually takes only weeks or a couple of months of practice.

No matter what the path to awakening, the person is left with a *knowing* and the ability to witness the activity of the conditioned mind. Perspectives are changed, perception is released by the ego, and intuitive knowledge suddenly becomes available in ways never before experienced. There is a definite feeling of "I've got it!" This is a fundamental and lasting change in one's "state of consciousness," not just a memory, in the untransformed consciousness, that has effects on perception.

Herein lays a grave danger. This "I've got it" knowing is exactly the door the ego needs to come back in and co-opt the entire awakening experience. The newly awakened awareness will be lost if the new life isn't supported through community, extensive study, and a dedication to this new-found path. Paul the Apostle didn't start teaching until fourteen years after his awakening experience on the road to Damascus. Where was he all that time? Reading, meditating, seeking, and deepening his insight.

As witnessing dominates, acceptance of "what is" takes hold. Surrender deepens. Forgiveness flourishes, and compassion floods the mind. This then is the path to the ultimate. Nisargadatta says, ". . . you must be extreme to reach the supreme."

Self-realization, by contrast to awakening is an act of grace. It happens spontaneously, unpredictably, and without volition. In fact, one of the last things that happens to many who realize enlightenment is giving up the spiritual search all together. The yearning for truth never goes away, but the understanding emerges that *trying* will not work – effort of any kind only moves one further away from the ultimate knowing. Effort comes from the ego-mind, the false self. Seeing this leaves the aspirant no alternative but to live life as it is given without any expectation of anything more. This surrender, giving up, and letting-go of the search itself is the last stage before we are captured by the true Self.

This ultimate dilemma, that of realizing that trying to move forward shifts the search into reverse, was captured eloquently by Steven Harrison in the title of his book, *Doing Nothing: Coming to the End of the Spiritual Search*.

Self-realization is really something we have no control over. But we can gradually sweep that which is false from our life. Witnessing thought is a powerful tool we have. We can study the mind. When we do, we find that we are a mechanism that is programmed by nature and nurture. We learn to see through the mind and the ego loses its authority over us.

We learn that our thoughts are not us. We learn that our self/personality isn't who we are either. We eventually learn that we are not our mind either. Nothing we can observe is who we are, including the body. We are nothing – no thing. Of course, seeing this is the final destruction of "we/me."

The great contemplative thinker and writer, Thomas Merton, described it this way;

> Since our innermost "I" is the perfect image of God, then, when that "I" awakens, he finds within himself the Presence of Him Whose image he is. And, by a paradox beyond all human expression, God and soul seem to have but one single "I." They are

(by divine grace) as though one single person. They breathe and live and act as one. "Neither" of the "two" is seen as object.

Behind that which is observed is no observer. There is only observing happening. There is no witness. There is only witnessing. No-thing, that which cannot be grasped with the mind, is watching. It cannot be understood by the mind, because the mind is contained within it. Infinite awareness in a Kingdom of No-thing in utter silence projecting the manifest universe for the simple pleasure of experiencing a Self – this is the cause of existence.
James Finley writes:

> We are "real" because we are in existence. God, however, is not in existence, but is rather Existence itself. He *is* that by which we are.

The world is God's mirror – made in God's image and likeness. When you look in the mirror, you don't see the real you, but you see the real *image* of you; noumenon becomes phenomenon. And God said, "Let there be light (Me)." And the un-manifested became manifested. This is what Jesus meant when he said,

> How shall we picture the kingdom of God, or by what parable shall we present it? It is like a mustard seed, which, when sown upon the soil, though it is smaller than all the seeds that are upon the soil, yet when it is sown, it grows up and becomes larger than all the garden plants and forms large branches; so that the birds of the air can nest under its shade.

The Awakening is the rebirth that leads to the ultimate understanding. This can happen in a variety of ways. Sometimes it is spontaneous. Sometimes it comes after months of labor and misery. The exercises in this book, as demonstrated by the various examples, are a road map to self-induced awakening. The literature is rife with caution about the vagaries of thought. Almost nowhere are instructions found on how to track down this interloper. The message of this book is simple and clear: There is an enemy at the gate. It is the source of all sorrow. Finding it, distinguishing it, and recognizing it will set you free.
It is the unprompted thought. It tells you what everything means. It filters reality. It hijacks the present. It is autopilot on a flight to hell. But it has a spokes-model, a public affairs director who can give you

secret access into the enemy's camp by following a well-worn trail. We need look no further.

To paraphrase Walt Kelly's *Pogo*, "We have met the enemy . . . and he is the voice in our head."

GENESIS REVISITED

So Adam and Eve eat from the Tree of the Knowledge of Good and Evil and are expelled from the Garden of Eden. The story goes that God sent powerful Cherubim to "keep" the way to the Tree of Life. The Tree of Life had the power to let Adam and Eve live forever. Now these Cherubim have flaming or enchanted swords. If you look carefully at the translation of the Hebrew word used here the word "flashing" might also be used. These swords flash in all directions! It is a common assumption that these creatures with their swords were supposed to keep humankind away from the Tree of Life. As I read it, it looks to me more like God is setting up a neon sign with an arrow pointing—"Eat at Joe's - Eternal Life Here!"

Let's go back to the brain for a moment. There is something very similar to the knowledge of good and evil and the basic function of the limbic system. It is the center of comparison, value judgment, criticizing, and making distinctions. Similarly, the Tree of Life reminds me of the prefrontal lobes – the portal of attention and alertness to *Now*. Could it be that the trees of Eden are analogous to the functions of these two brain structures? Could it be that the Tree of Eternal Life has been there all along? That all we ever had to do was to look and pay attention?

Figure 16-1 The Tree of Life and the Tree of the Knowledge of Good and Evil

". . . and he placed at the east of the Garden of Eden trusted assistants holding a neon sign which rotated, to show the direction to the Tree of Life." We've been looking at it all this time. We just didn't see it because it was so obvious.

Chapter 17: Final Perspectives

When there is no personal self, there is no personal God

Bernadette Roberts

PAT'S PERSPECTIVE:

I have to admit that I'm more than just a little uncomfortable with the way this turned out. I don't know where this bliss came from that I felt. I would have had no idea that it has existed inside of me the whole time, and that the only reason I couldn't feel it was that I misidentified everything. I mean, I understand the exercises and it all makes sense, but whoa! This is a little scary. This not really knowing who you really are – it's spooky.

But no matter what Dr. Mark's philosophy is or how it affects me, I'm still going to watch my thoughts. I never did experience the bliss in exactly the same way I did on that one glorious day, but I have a growing sense of it there, inside me. It seems subtle, but I know the feeling of it. It just doesn't blow me away the way it did that particular day. This is probably because now I'm acquainted with it and the feeling of peace and joy isn't such a shock to me.

Anyway, back to the thought-watching thing. I lost my job a few months ago, and I was out of work for two months. My mind wanted to make everything a drama. The thoughts bombarded me: "I'm a failure." "I'm no good." "I'll never be successful." You know what I mean. It went on and on. I wasn't perfect at watching my thoughts, but whenever I stayed in witness consciousness, the thoughts disappeared, and I would remain unaffected. It was a bit of a battle to keep doing it. All the messages from my childhood— my father's expectations, the messages I got about what it means to be a man from TV, society – they all tried to play in my head. When I stood fast as the *witness*, nothing touched me. When I bought in to the drama, I would immediately be discouraged and depressed and start feeling sorry for myself. It was drama, drama, nothing but drama. Not one of those thoughts helped me get a job faster.

So I learned the lesson of witnessing at an even deeper level. I could really see how thought-identification was a vicious trap of insanity. But that wasn't all I was able to see.

I began to ask myself every time I had a reaction, "How is this related to my father?" I was astounded. My programmed, conditioned mind thinks that everything is related to my father. In a very real sense, it thinks the world is dad. I never realized how deep the trance of the conditioned mind really is.

I have to say that at first all of this was subtle. It's not now. Now that I'm used to looking at my mind from the perspective of awareness, these things stand out in bas-relief. I have no trouble at all spotting the activity of the mind. But as I say, this whole thing of *me* not being real and everything being one or unity, that makes me a little queasy. It's not so much that I don't believe it. It's just that it feels real safe as long as it's only a philosophy. But when you stand in a mirror and try to realize the implications of it, the world starts spinning. I'm not sure I'm ready for that level of detachment.

I noticed that my last statement was made around the reference point of *safety*. Well I'm a Unicorn, and watching my thoughts and my conditioned patterns has shown me how relentlessly my mind hangs on to safety. I only bring that up because I want to make a few comments on how all of this has affected my relationship with Angie. When I felt like I was really in that new level of consciousness that Dr. Mark calls *witness consciousness*, I went back and looked at this whole Lion/Unicorn theory of his. I must admit, I was even more blown away than the first time I was exposed to it.

It is not so much that I saw how true it was in all cases and for all people. It just really helped me as a road map for my experience. My witnessing of thought became even sharper because I knew what to look for. But that wasn't the biggest benefit.

I am now continuously aware of my Unicorn mind at work during my interactions with Angie. I can see the tendencies to seek safety, to avoid, to passively resist, and to punish her by withholding. Now, I'm not always perfect at catching these tendencies right away; but I have to give myself some credit here. Being the *watcher* when I'm around her has totally transformed our relationship. We really now have the same feeling between us that we did when we first met. And there is a depth to it that we never had before. There really is a sense of partnership and for me—comfort, and calm.

Oh, yes, she gets upset once in a while. But most of the time I look inside and see my reaction to it long before it turns into acting out. I accept her exactly the way she is, and I try not to identify with thoughts that she needs to change in any way. I am especially on guard for my objection to her anger. I know that's completely about me. Well, this allows me to move in close to her and give her the love and reassurance I know she never got that produced those patterns in her in the first place. When she comes out of the reaction, there is always a review and reconciliation. We both know that this is our ego-mind at work, and so we let it go and go back to being conscious with one another. Life is ever so much easier without the drama of identification.

Witness consciousness really is a whole new lease on life. I know Dr. Mark wouldn't call what we did therapy in the strictest sense. But I'm very glad that he knew what had happened to me and was willing to take the risk to bring me the rest of the way.

ANGIE'S PERSPECTIVE:

Well, I guess I have a little different perspective on all this than Pat does. Since I'm a Lion, I'm willing to go "where angels fear to tread," so to speak. Anyway, I want the whole thing – the whole enchilada. What I mean is that I want self-realization or whatever you want to call it. I don't want to spend any more of my life in this false hell. So you know what I've been doing? I've been reading, I've been surfing the web, I'm scooping up any bit of information I can to try and take the next step.

You know, that sounds funny because it's such a dilemma. I know that I can't get closer to enlightenment by "trying" but I'm so hungry, consumed almost, that I will do anything. So be it. Anyway, the reason I'm consuming so much information is that I feel if such and such a teacher says it a little differently, I will understand it better.

But the biggest tool of all is the Awakening of Witness Consciousness. I realize now that I had read or heard some of what Mark was saying before. But I never could really understand it. Oh, it went into my head alright, but you know how much value head-knowledge has. Now that I am in awareness instead of my head, I really do understand so much more of the literature of enlightenment.

Even in the midst of all of this "effort" I'm learning something so interesting it blows me away. I'm not the *doer*. Dr. Mark had been telling me this. And so I experimented with it. I found that my sense of doing comes after the *doingness* has been initiated. Damn! My ego-mind wants to take credit for what I do, but it comes after the doing has started. Believe it or not, this discovery has taken a lot of pressure off me. There is no free will. Life is an E-ticket so I'm just going to take the ride and enjoy. But can you imagine that we're so arrogant that we want to take credit for what we *do,* but we only know we do it about a half second after the doing starts? So the ego is like this giant interpreter of life – telling us what everything means and pretending like we're the producer/director of the action.

I can tell you that this experience with Dr. Mark has left me a lot more humble than I was before. The first time we went to him was bad enough. I had to take a look at my Lion tendencies, my arrogance, and all my bullshit. It wasn't a pretty picture. This time it was even worse, but much better in a way. It was worse in the respect that I discovered the truth about myself. I am nothing! I don't exist in the way I've always believed I do. Here I've been going around trying to sell my *act* to everyone, only to find out by direct experience that the separate person with this delightful persona doesn't exist as such. Oh! My God!

It kind of takes the stuffing out of you. But then you realize what's really behind it all. Once the deception of the ego-mind is swept away and collapses, we discover ourselves as that eternal presence that is Existence itself. I want that, and I won't rest until I get it. Saying that, I am painfully aware that struggling won't make it happen. I do know there is a moment of surrender that comes, but I'm not there yet. So for now I'm just going to enjoy immersing myself into this whole Self-discovery thing with all the gusto I've got.

This has all made me study my mind even more closely. It all started with my discovery of myself as a Lion. Shame was all I knew. I didn't believe anybody loved me, cared, or saw me as special in any way. I really have been able to drop all of that. Witnessing is what allowed me to do it. When I learned to watch my thoughts, I really could see how much of this neediness had invaded my mind. It dominated every second of my day. All I could think about was how I could get Pat to be more loving and caring. I see now how much I was sucking the air right out of his lungs. Today we laugh about it. We're just having the best time!

In the midst of all of this, I found my passion. I realize now that my psychic energy was all tied up in my anger. I had such enormous defensiveness around my pain of not being good enough. Anyway, it turns out that when the falseness of that service to pain was swept away, a profound need to help other people travel the path of Self-discovery emerged. I want to be a teacher. I want to share with others what I've discovered and help them discover freedom themselves.

This world revolves around ego-drama. I was reading a book called *I Am That* that Mark recommended to me by an Indian fellow, Nisargadatta Maharaj. In it he says the ego is like a rope across a road. All it does is snarl traffic. Boy, that's for sure! I would really like to play a role in helping others see that. I also know that it has to happen one person at a time. I hope I get the chance to spread the word.

MARK'S PERSPECTIVE:

Let me begin by saying that you don't have to swallow this book whole and choke on it in the process. For me there are several key concepts that are more important to accept and the rest will come, if it's supposed to, for each reader. The fact that we are under the spell of the ego-mind, limbic system, five-year-old cannot be overlooked. The trance state that this produces is far more extensive than science has ever understood. So that's the first big idea that must open our eyes to our mechanistic, robotic lives.

The next big idea is that of the dialogical self, this voice in our heads. The fact that we can actually watch it and dis-identify with it is a radical idea whose time has come. This voice in our heads is not under our control and is ruining our lives. This leads to the whole concept of *witness consciousness*. Once a person moves into that area of detachment from programmed thought, most psychological problems become accessible for eradication. Problem resolution is spontaneous, but with a little coaching the rest is easy.

This leads to another key theme. Since the ego-mind works based on association, it is relatively easy to trigger the problem-system while the person watches from the perspective of the witness. This is a new kind of psychotherapy. I have literally seen clients resolve lifelong issues in a few sessions. It is time for the helping professions to embrace this concept and move away from advice-giving, assaulting defenses, and drama reenactment—all of which have proven to have a poor track record for people's lives. As Einstein said, "No problem can be solved from the same level of consciousness that created it. We must see the world anew."

So, for me, these are the important first two levels of this work. This is a template for healing and awareness. Even if someone doesn't move on from there, the benefits are astonishing. This literally frees a person from generations of darkness. As I said in earlier chapters, once experienced, *witness consciousness* must be supported so as not to have it hijacked by the ego.

This is the Awakening brought about by exposing the voice of the ego-mind.

That being said, this opening in awareness serves the purpose of revealing the path home to the true Self. For those who choose this path, there is a yearning and hunger for the final realization. I see Angie on this path. Pat is somewhat hesitant. I understand this. It is like a free fall. We lose all of our familiar reference points, including ourselves!

Amit Goswami says in *THE SELF AWARE UNIVERSE*:

> *Most people, lost in the illusion of their ego-separateness and busy in its pursuits, are not motivated to discover truth themselves. How then can the light of the mystic's realization be shared with these people? The answer is to simplify it.*

It may not seem that what I've said in this book simplifies much. And yet that has been my aim. The structure and function of the brain itself, when revealed by research, is compelling. But I am a psychotherapist. During the writing of this book I had a dialogue via e-mail with one of these brain theorists. My point to him was that since the limbic system is developmentally so much ahead of the prefrontal lobes, would it be right to assume that the limbic system holds sway over the dialogical self. Oh, no, he told me. That would be too simple. It's much more complicated than that.

Frankly, this response stymied me for a couple of days. I was almost despondent. How could he not see what to me was so obvious? I walked out of my office one night after a particularly gratifying session with a delightful couple. Suddenly it hit me. These researchers don't see it because they don't work with people all day long. It's not complicated. In fact, it's even simpler than we might ever have suspected. I had to learn to trust my instincts.

So in writing this book, I've taken one giant leap after another. I have taken fact, as verified by research, to a logical conclusion that is inescapable for someone who does marriage counseling and psychotherapy.

And what's been extraordinarily gratifying is how readily my clients have taken to the principles. I've presented my ideas to them in much the same way as you read them in this book. My Pats and Angies have said a resounding *Yes.* The have dug into the work, done the exercises, and come back changed. Why? Because it seemed too simple not to be true. Then they proved it in their lives.

The fact of the human condition is amazingly simple, astoundingly simple.

It reminds me of the client who looked at me in surprise one day and said, "No wonder I couldn't see it. It was too obvious."

The simple fact is that we have been hijacked by the limbic system. Our every thought, perception, feeling, and reaction is driven by a trance state so powerful and yet so familiar that it feels like normal life to us. But the emperor has no clothes.

This hijacking creates a deception that has kept us from our rightful inheritance of life. We are not earning our way to some pie in the sky. We are the pie! Paul in Ephesians says that marriage creates "one flesh" between a man and a woman. Then he says that he is really revealing a great mystery concerning Christ and the church. What is the mystery? ONE, we are one, not separate little "me's" running around.

James Finley related his awakening experience during a workshop I attended. He talked about feeling like he was breathing God. This breathing-God experience went on for three days. Why? Because we *are* breathing God! The essence of every breath is God. It is the reality that our conditioned ego-mind doesn't want us to see because IT wants to be God.

Exposing the voice of the ego-mind reveals the ultimate deception and our chance finally to discover the true Self. It is amazingly simple; all we have to do is look.

Bibliography

Abraham, D. J. (2004). *The Quest for the Spiritual Neuron.* Koramangala, India: National Printing Press.

Adamson, "Sailor" B. (2004). *Just This and Nothing Else: Presence - Awareness.* (J. Wheeler, Ed.) Salisbury, UK: Non-Duality Press.

Adamson, "Sailor" B. (2004). *What's Wrong with Right Now?* Salisbury, UK: Non-Duality Press.

Amit Goswami, P. (1995). *The Self-Aware Universe.* New York: Putnam.

Andrew Newberg, M. E. (2001). *Why God Won't Go Away.* New York: Ballantine.

Arthur Becker-Weidman, P. (n.d.). *Child Abuse and Neglect.* Retrieved from http://www.mental-health-matters.com: http://www.mental-health-matters.com/articles/article.php?artID=581.

Austin, James H. (2000). *Zen and the Brain.* Cambridge, MA: MIT Press.

Balsekar, R. (1982). *Pointers From Nisargadatta Maharaj.* Durham, NC: Acorn Press.

Balsekar, R. (1989). *A Duet of One: The Ashtavakra Gita Dialogue.* Los Angeles: Advaita Press.

Balsekar, R. (2002). *The Ultimate Understanding.* London: Watkins Publishing.

Chopra, D. (2000). *How to Know God.* New York: Three Rivers Press.

Courtney, A. (2004). *Resting in the Cave of the Heart.* Orinda, CA: DreamBooks Publishing.

D'Esposito, C. R. (2005). Directing the mind's eye: prefrontal, inferior and medial temporal mechanisms for visual working memory. *Current Opinion in*

Awakening

Neurobiology, 15, 175–182.

Damasio, A. (1994). *Descartes' Error.* New York: G.P. Putnam's Sons.

Damasio, A. (1999). *The Feeling of What Happens.* New York: Harcourt Brace and Company.

Damasio, A. (2003). *Looking for Spinoza.* New York: Harcourt, Inc.

David Hawkins, M. P. (2001). *The Eye of the I.* W. Sedona, AZ: Veritas.

David Hawkins, M. P. (2003). *Reality and Subjectivity.* W. Sedona, AZ: Veritas.

Davidson, H. H. (2004). Disambiguating the Components of Emotional Regulation. *Child Development, 75* (2), 361-365.

Davidson, R. J. (2004). What does the prefrontal cortex "do" in affect: perspectives on frontal EEG asymmetry research. *Biological Psychology, 67,* 219–233.

Davidson R. J (2004). The privileged status of emotion in the brain. *The Proceedings of the National Academy of Sciences, 101* (33), 11915–11916.

Davis, K. (2004). *Awake Living Joy.* Kihei, HI: Manuscript.

D'Esposito, B. R. (1999). The roles of prefrontal brain regions in components of working memory: Effects of memory load and individual differences. *Proceedings of the National Accademy of Sciences, 96* (11), 6558-6563.

Eckhart, M. (1994). *Selected Writings.* New York: Penguin.

Finley, J. (1978). *Merton's Palace of Nowhere.* Notre Dame, IN: Ave Maria Press.

Finley, J. (2000). *The Contemplative Heart.* Notre Dame, IN: Sorin Books.

Freeman, W. J. (n.d.). *Emotion is Essential to All Intentional Behaviors.* Retrieved from http://sulcus.berkeley.edu: http://sulcus.berkeley.edu/wjf/CE. Neurodynamics.and.Emotion.pdf.

Freeman, W. J. (n.d.). *Walter J. Freeman*. Retrieved from Walter J. Freeman: http://sulcus.berkeley.edu.

Freeman, W. J. (2000). Perception of time and causation through the kinesthesia of intentional action. *Cognitive Processing, 1.*

Freeman, W. J. (2001). Bridging the Gaps Between Neuron, Brain and Behavior with Neurodynamics. *Jean Piaget Society Symposium.* Berkeley, CA.

Freeman, W. J. (2001). *How Brains Make Up Their Minds* . New York: Columbia University Press.

Freeman, W. J. (2004). *Mass Action in the Nervous System.* New York: Academic Press.

Gangaji. (1995). *You Are That.* Boulder, CO: Satsang Press.

Gangaji. (1999). *Freedom & Resolve.* Ashland, OR: The Gangaji Foundation.

Greenberger, D. & Padesky, C. (1995). *Mind Over Mood.* New York: The Guilford Press.

Gunaratana, H. (1991). *Mindfulness in Plain English.* Boston: Wisdom Publications.

Harding, D. (2000). *Face to No Face.* (D. Lang, Ed.) San Diego, CA: Inner Directions.

Harding, D. (1998). *Look for Yourself.* San Diego, CA: Inner Directions.

Harding, D. (2002). *On Having No Head.* San Diego, CA: Inner Directions.

Harrison, S. (1997). *Doing Nothing: Coming to the End of the Spritual Search.* New York: Putnam.

Harrison, S. (1999). *Being One*, Boulder, CO: Sentient Publications

Awakening

Harrison, S. (2002). *The Question to Life's Answers*. Boulder, CO: Sentient Publications.

Helena Matute, M. A. (n.d.). *Inferring Causality and Making Predictions. Some Misconceptions in the Animal and Human Learning Literature*. Retrieved from www.interdisciplines.org: http://www.interdisciplines.org/causality/papers/16.

Hermans, H. J. (2002). The Dialogical Self as a Society of Mind: Introduction. *Theory & Psychology, 12* (2), 147–160.

Hiroshi Yamasaki, K. S. (2002). Dissociable prefrontal brain systems for attention and emotion. *Proceedings of the National Accademy of Sciences, 99* (17), 11447–11451.

Jacobson, L. (1991). *Words from Silence*. La Selva Beach, CA: Conscious Living.

Jacobson, L. (1997). *Embracing the Present*. La Selva Beach, CA: Conscious Living.

Jacobson, L. (1999). *Bridging Heaven & Earth*. La Selva Beach, CA: Conscious Living.

Jaxon-Bear, E. (2004). *Sudden Awakening*. Novato, CA: H.J. Kramer.

Jaynes, J. (1976). *The Origin of Consciousness in the Breakdown of the Bicameral Mind*. Boston: Houghton Mifflin.

Johnston, V. (1999). *Why We Feel: The Science of Human Emotions*. Cambridge, MA: Helix.

Jourdain, S. (2001). *Radical Awakening*. (G. Farcet, Ed.) San Diego, CA: Inner Directions.

Kabat-Zinn, J. (1991). *Full Catastrophe Living*. New York: Bantam, Doubleday, Dell

Kline, John P., J. J. (1998). Is Left Frontal Brain Activation in Defensiveness Gender Specific? *Journal of Abnormal Psychology, 107* (1), 149-153.

Kornfield, J. (1993). *A Path with Heart.* New York: Bantam.

Kornfield, J. (2000). *After the Ecstasy, the Laundry.* New York: Bantam.

Krishnamurti, U. (2002). *The Mystique of Enlightenment.* Boulder, CO: Sentient Publications.

Lars Martensson, M. (1997, September 16th). LOVE, HOPE, & BRAIN SCIENCE. *Based on a public lecture at the University of Oslo.* Oslo, Norway.

Lewis, M. D. (2002). The Dialogical Brain: Contributions of Emotional Neurobiology to Understanding the Dialogical Self. *Theory & Psychology, 12* (2), 175-190.

Libet, B. (2005). *Mind Time: The Temporal Factor in Consciousness (Perspectives in Cognitive Neuroscience).* Cambridge, MA: Harvard University Press

Maharaj, S. N. (1987). *The Nectar of Immortality.* (P. Robert Powell, Ed.) San Diego, CA: Blue Dove.

Maharaj, S. N. (1990). *I Am That: Talks with Sri Nisargadatta.* Durham, NC: Acorn Press.

Maharaj, S. N. (1994). *Consciousness and the Absolute.* (J. Dunn, Ed.) Durham, NC: Acorn Press.

Maharaj, S. N. (1994). *The Ultimate Medicine.* (P. Robert Powell, Ed.) San Diego, CA: Blue Dove Press.

Maharaj, S. N. (2001). *The Experience of Nothingness.* (P. Robert Powell., Ed.) San Diego, CA: Blue Dove Press.

Maharsh, R. (1992). *Be as You Are: The Teachings of Sri Ramana Maharshi.* (D. Godman, Ed.) New Delhi: Penguin India.

Maharshi, R. (2000). *Talks with Ramana Maharshi.* San Diego, CA: Inner Directions.

McKenna, J. (2002). *Spiritual Enlightenment: The Damndest Thing.* Wisefool Press.

Merton, T. (1955). *No Man Is An Island.* New York: Harcourt Brace and Company.

Mitchell, S. (1992). *Tao te Ching.* New York: Harper Perennial.

Mitchell, S. (1998). *The Essence of Wisdom.* New York: Broadway Books.

Mitchell, S. (2000). *Bhagavad Gita.* New York: Three Rivers Press.

Morrison, S. (1992). *Open and Innocent.* Atlanta, GA: American Zen Society Press.

Ouspensky, P. (1949). *In Search of the Miraculous.* New York: Harcourt Brace & Company.

Ouspensky, P. (1971). *The Fourth Way.* New York: Vintage.

Parsons, T. (2000). *As It Is.* San Diego, CA: Inner Directions.

Parsons, T. (2004). *Invitation to Awaken.* San Diego, CA: Inner Directions.

Paul Watzlawick, P. J. (1974). *Change.* New York: W. W. Norton.

Perry, R. (1997). *Relationships as a Spiritual Journey.* West Sedona, AZ: The Circle of Atonement Teaching and Healing Center

Pinker, S. (1997). *How the Mind Works.* New York: W. W. Norton.

Roberts, B. (1985). *The Path to No-Self.* Boston: Shambala.

Roberts, B. (1993). *The Experience of No-Self.* Albany: State of New York Press.

Rogers, L. (2001). *Sexing the Brain.* New York: Columbia University Press.

Rose, R. (1973). *The Albigen Papers.* Benwood, WV: TAT Foundation.

Rose, R. (1979). *Psychology of the Observer.* Benwood, WV: TAT Foundation.

Rose, R. (1985). *The Direct-Mind Experience.* Benwood, WV: TAT Foundation.

Rosenberg, L. (1999). *Breath by Breath.* Boston: Shambhala.

Shallice, T. (2001). Theory of mind and the prefrontal cortex. *Brain, 124* (2), 247–248.

Schucman, H. & Thetford, W. (1976). *A Course in Miracles.* Glen Ellen, CA: Foundation for Inner Peace.

Siegel, D. (1999). *The Developing Mind.* New York: Guilford Press.

Terrell, A. (1997). *Surprised by Grace.* Boulder, CO. True Light Publishing

Tolle, E. (1999). *The Power of Now.* Novato: New World Library.

Tollifson, J. (2003). *Awake in the Heartland.* Victoria, BC: Trafford.

Tononi, E. &. (2000). *A Universe of Consciousness.* New York: Basic Books.

Valsiner, J. (2002). Forms of Dialogical Relations and Semiotic Autoregulation within the Self. *Theory & Psychology, 12* (2), 251–265 .

Wei, W. W. (1964). *All Else Is Bondage.* Fairfield, IA: Sunstar.

Wei, W. W. (2002). *Ask the Awakened.* Boulder, CO: Sentient Publications.

Wei, W. W. (2003). *Fingers Pointing Towards the Moon.* Boulder, CO: Sentient Publications.

Wei, W. W. (2003). *The Tenth Man.* Boulder, CO: Sentient Publications.

Wei, W. W. (2003). *Why Lazarus Laughed.* Boulder, CO: Sentient Publications.

Wei, W. W. (2004). *Open Secret.* Boulder, CO: Sentient Publications.

Welwood, J. (1996). *Love and Awakening.* New York: HarperPerennial.

Welwood, J. (2000). *Toward a Psychology of Awakening.* Boston: Shambala.

White, M. & Epston, D. (1990). *Narrative Means to Therapeutic Ends.* New York: W.W. Norton & Company

William Irwin, M. J. (2004). Amygdalar interhemispheric functional connectivity differs between. *NeuroImage, 21,* 674–686.

Williams LM, L. B. (n.d.). Amygdala-prefrontal dissociation of subliminal and supraliminal fear. *Brain Net.*

Glossary

afference, preafference, preafferent: Afference describes the mechanism of information coming in from the outer sensory system of the body into the processing centers of the brain. Preafference means before information is transmitted.

Amygdala: Cherry-shaped objects buried in the temporal lobes that are part of the limbic system of the brain. The main job of the amygdala is to process emotions.

association cortexes: Wide areas of the brain involved in memory of various types.

attractor pattern: Attractors appear by graphing phase space, which is beyond normal linear mathematical relationships. Attractor fields, pattern, or "strange" attractors are highly organized energy fields that tend to pull everything in a given system toward themselves.

awakened: The property of having perception freed of preconceptions. Being out of the dream of the conditioned mind.

awareness: Conscious knowing.

cerebral cortex: The outer, folded, surface of the brain.

chaos theory: The name comes from the observation that some systems that are apparently disordered have an underlying order in apparently random data.

consciousness: Awareness, but used as a noun.

content vs. process: Content is the *story* while process is the *how*.

defenses: Those things we do to protect ourselves from a percieved attack.

dialogical self: The voice in your head. This is sometimes multiple voices.

Awakening

disowned part, parts: Aspects of our personality that we do not want to see or admit that we have.

enlightenment: Having appropriated the final understanding of the mystery of life.

Hippocampus: A part of the limbic system critical in memory and processing our sense of space and time.

identification: Attributing one's self to something other than the attributor.

identified thinker: A person who identifies themself with the content of their thoughts.

introjects: Incorporate or assimilate into one's self aspects of representations of others, especially parents.

lesion: An injury to the brain.

limbic system: A primitive part of the brain mainly concerned with survival of the organisim.

mind: A label placed on discernable activity of the brain and nervous system.

natural state: See enlightenment.

perception: A *representation* of sensory and nonsensory input from the brain.

personality: Goal-directed emotional states that bundled together we identify as ourselves.

preafference: See "afference."

prefrontal cortex, lobes: That part of the brain near the forehead.

prefrontals: My shorthand for the above.

presence: The sensation of consciousness or awareness.

process: See "content."

Repetition compulsion: One's tendency to repeat traumatic events in order to deal with them.

Ritualistic reenactment: The tendency to recreate thematically experiences of early childhood.

self-observation: The ability to see our motivations and behaviors.

struggle: Our *doingness* that propels us toward some emotionally laden goal.

sub-personalities: Goal-directed emotional states targeted toward narrowly focused aspects of the personality.

trance: The property of being benumbed by our programming into thinking what we are experiencing is similar to another experience.

Index

A

C

D

E

H

I

identification vi, 26, 55, 66, 71, 72, 74, 76, 78, 89, 91, 93, 96, 105, 106,
107, 115, 122, 128, 132, 133, 134, 135, 139, 140, 141, 142, 143, 144,
152, 153, 170, 173
identified thinker vi, 78, 86, 88, 89, 93, 94, 128, 135, 143, 170, 173
introjects 81, 82, 83, 170, 173

L

lesion 30, 170, 173
limbic system 5, 6, 10, 13, 14, 17, 35, 38, 39, 41, 47, 48, 49, 50, 51, 52, 53,
54, 55, 64, 65, 67, 68, 73, 74, 75, 80, 83, 85, 86, 88, 89, 92, 95, 96,
97, 108, 109, 112, 113, 114, 117, 139, 140, 141, 148, 155, 156, 157,
169, 170, 173

M

mind ii, xi, xii, xiii, xiv, xv, 1, 3, 4, 5, 6, 7, 9, 10, 18, 23, 24, 25, 26, 29, 32,
34, 37, 38, 40, 43, 44, 47, 51, 55, 57, 58, 59, 60, 61, 62, 66, 71, 72,
73, 74, 76, 77, 78, 79, 81, 82, 83, 84, 85, 86, 87, 90, 91, 92, 93, 94,
95, 96, 97, 101, 102, 104, 105, 106, 108, 109, 112, 113, 114, 116, 117,
120, 121, 122, 125, 128, 131, 132, 133, 134, 135, 137, 139, 140, 141,
142, 143, 144, 145, 146, 147, 151, 152, 153, 154, 155, 156, 157, 160,
166, 169, 170, 173

N

natural state 9, 10, 170, 174

P

Perception i, ii, 50, 51, 58, 65, 102, 161, 174
personality 74, 80, 81, 83, 130, 133, 135, 137, 140, 141, 142, 143, 145, 146,
170, 171, 174
Preafference i, ii, 47, 51, 169, 174
preafference 52, 65, 169, 171, 174
preafferent 51, 54, 65, 67, 100, 169, 174
prefrontal v, 14, 30, 31, 32, 33, 34, 36, 57, 67, 68, 73, 74, 89, 96, 103, 135,
148, 156, 160, 162, 166, 167, 171, 174
prefrontal cortex 14, 34, 36, 160, 166, 171, 174
prefrontal lobes v, 14, 30, 31, 32, 33, 34, 36, 57, 67, 68, 73, 74, 89, 96, 103,
135, 148, 156, 174
prefrontals 29, 30, 31, 32, 33, 34, 73, 171, 174

About Mark Waller

PROFESSIONAL PROFILE:
Mark Waller is an award winning author of four books and numerous articles. A licensed Marriage and Family Therapist, he has been a management consultant for over ten years and has conducted workshops for manufacturers, utilities, and the computer industry. He has lectured at the University of Wisconsin and George Washington University. Mark has a B.A. in Business, a Masters Degree in Counseling, and a Ph.D. in Psychology. He has extensive experience helping executives and couples, as well as groups.

Mark is a highly respected clinician and professional with a worldwide reputation for his interpersonal and communications skills. He is a demonstrated leader and innovator who is a professional platform speaker/trainer and has a proven track record of achievement in sales and marketing.

PERSONAL PROFILE:
Mark Waller had a midlife crisis and became a statistic. At 40, he was a successful technical consultant, and the author of three books on computers and electrical power. His first book was entitled *Computer Electrical Power Requirements*. His second book, *PC Power Protection*, was a Tab Book Club main selection. His third book, *Mark Waller's Harmonics*, established him as an acknowledged leader in the field of electrical power quality. He received The Award of Achievement from the Society of Technical Communications in the 1988–89 competition for an article written for *Byte Magazine*. At that time, he was named a "Finalist" in L. Ron Hubbard's "Writers of the Future" contest (he is not a Scientologist). He traveled the country giving workshops and consulting for companies such as Southern California Edison and The Jet Propulsion Laboratory. He taught classes at Georgetown University and the University of Wisconsin.

Then disaster struck. The economy, the marriage, and the lifestyle all collapsed at the same time. Mark had nothing left but pain and fear. During this dark night of the soul Mark experienced an *awakening*. This led to a career and life change. His next book, THE DANCE OF THE LION AND THE UNICORN, was born from new insight that followed.

Today Mark is a Licensed Marriage and Family Therapist in Southern California where he lives with his wife Sheila. His passion is helping others experience *awakening* as well.

Reader Survey

Please circle one answer.

Did you enjoy my book, *AWAKENING*?　　　　　Yes　　　　No
Please explain why or why not _____

_____

_____

Was it helpful?　　　　　　　　　　　　Yes　　　　No
Did you learn anything new?　　　　　　　　Yes　　　　No
Could you relate it to your own life or experience?　Yes　　　　No
Did it make you want to take action?　　　　Yes　　　　No

What was your favorite part or concept? _____

_____

_____

Do you have any additional comments? _____

_____

_____

Would you be willing to write a review to be posted on Amazon.com? If so please go to their site and look up my book. Links for review submission are clearly posted. Thank you very much!

Can we add you to our e-mail newsletter list? Please print legibly.

_____

Would you like to be notified when Mark Waller comes to your area for a workshop or book signing? *Please make sure you give us your e-mail address.*

_____　　　　　Yes　　　　No

Please fill out and mail to:　　　　Or scan and e-mail as an image file to:
Mark Waller　　　　　　　　　　　　　mail@markwaller.com
4195 Chino Hills Pkwy PMB 611　　　　For more information go to
Chino Hills, Ca 917098　　　　　　　　www.markwaller.com

Printed in the United States
74238LV00005B/142